Prospecting with Purpose

How to Methodically Grow Your Real Estate Business

by Shannon Ensor

Prospecting with Purpose

How to Methodically Grow Your Real Estate Business

ISBN-13: 978-0-9970862-3-2

Cover by Adazing
Edited by Clear Voice Editing, Lori Handelman, PhD
Interior Design by Hector Elias at The Book Architect

Jands Publishing
Job 42:2

www.ShannonEnsor.com

Twitter: @shannon_ensor

Printed in the United States of America
First Printing, September 2016

Prospecting with Purpose

How to Methodically Grow Your Real Estate Business

Contents

Introduction

A FEW YEARS AGO MY COMPANY EXPANDED and I took on a handful of new-to-me agents. They came to me frustrated and ragged, but also hungry to succeed in this business. After a few meetings with them, I could see it was their lack of prospecting for new clients that was holding them back in their careers. Some felt as though they were prospecting, as they had participated in various and expensive lead generation programs, but with little or no success. None had a machine in place—a system that would consistently help them prospect for new clients and succeed in this business.

So I created a class for them. I analyzed what I had done in my career to become successful, and it became obvious: my success came from working several components concurrently, as opposed to trying one area until it failed and moving on to the next. I placed these components into a pie graph on a handout for my class, and laughed at its resemblance to a game piece in Trivial Pursuit™. (I even found a super-fancy font that resembled the one on the board game and labeled the handout "Real Estate Trivial Pursuit"!) Right there on that handout was my real estate machine: the six parts, almost equal to each other, that kept my business running smoothly.

That next day in class I saw light bulbs appear over the new agents' heads as the six components were laid out for them. I urged them to stop spending time on one section of the pie and ignoring the rest until they became desperate again—their previous business cycle—and instead to focus almost equally on all components at the same time. This was a game changer for these agents.

Now, any time I see an agent on my team slipping back into the cycle of frustration, I pull her aside and we analyze where she is investing her time and identify which areas she has been ignoring—which cogs of her machine aren't running efficiently. Sometimes all it takes is a little tweaking and her machine is back up and running smoothly again.

With the popularity of groups on Facebook and other online forums, I am exposed to agents all over the world who cry for help with their careers. New and experienced agents alike plead for direction, just like the agents I take onto my team. I have created this book for them, and for you. No matter how many years you have been in this business, I am confident you will learn how to boost your career with this book. Even the most successful agents can have areas of weakness in their business. This book will help eradicate those weak areas and propel your success to greater levels.

In the chapters to come I'm going to walk you through the six primary components of your business that are key to prospecting, discuss why you need each one, and show how you can leverage each component into the others. I will also discuss other prospecting tactics that you can implement for increased success, and I'll tell you when something should be used sparingly so that you can be a more efficient agent. But first, you must believe you can become a successful agent and that you possess the grit it takes to succeed in this business. There is no overnight success in real estate, and each top-producing agent you admire has put in the hard work necessary to get to the top. You must do the same.

I encourage you to highlight sections in this book and dog-ear the pages that speak to you the most. Like me and every other agent on this planet, you are human and may find yourself slipping back into old habits that take you off track. When that happens, pick up this book once again and revisit those highlights and dog-ears and refresh yourself on the systems that once yielded success for you. I'm arming you with the guidebook that will improve your career, but you are responsible for applying the principles.

Most importantly, I believe that your time is valuable. For this reason, you may find me a little more cut-to-the-chase than rah-rah. There are many successful books available that can get you pumped up about being an agent. We agents are typically self-motivators, so the occasional cheerleading fuels us. However, in this book, you're not going to find any fluff. Instead, you'll find every secret, strategy and tip that I can fit into this book—no dangling secrets that keep you wondering what you should do to succeed. I'll hold nothing back. I believe real estate should be a tangible career for everyone who is willing to put in the work.

My goal is to give you a clear direction for your real estate career. When you know what components to focus on in your business, your approach becomes clear and your frustration dissolves. Dive in and discover how to methodically grow your real estate business through purposeful prospecting!

Glossary

IF REAL ESTATE IS A NEW CAREER FOR YOU, I'd like to introduce you to some common terms and real estate jargon you will see abbreviated throughout the book.

COE: REALTOR® Code of Ethics

CTA: Call to Action. This is the most critical part of any marketing piece because it moves your specified audience to contact you from your marketing.

Expired(s): Home that recently went off the MLS system because the prior listing agent's agreement expired.

Farm(ing): Geographic area an agent chooses to target

FSBO: For Sale by Owner. Seller wants to sell without an agent's representation, though will in many cases allow and pay a buyer's agent.

IDX: Internet Data Exchange. This allows websites, whether the big national players or your own, to receive a feed of listings from the MLS system.

MCE:	Mandatory Continuing Education
MLS:	Multiple Listing Service. A database and software used by real estate agents to share listing information with other brokers.
SOI:	Sphere of Influence. The people who already know and (hopefully) like you. Typically an agent's go-to for business, especially when newly licensed.

Chapter 1
Real Estate Trivial Pursuit

As mentioned in the beginning of the book, I created a class for my struggling agents called Real Estate Trivial Pursuit™. Not trivial at all, this concept organizes the six major components of a real estate business and applies the popular board game's rules in that you have to complete all pieces of your pie in order to win the game.

Without further ado, the six main components of an agent's career that must be focused on for a well-rounded business are:

- Buyers and sellers: This is actually working with your clients and getting to the closing table.
- Database: The people who know you and already recognize you as a real estate agent (or will soon).
- Farming: Farming is a key component to neighborhood dominance and a long life in this business.
- Open houses: Open houses are critical to gaining leads and growing your database, and contribute to neighborhood dominance.

- Internet/social media: This includes everything online—your personal website, social media sites, and even video.
- FSBOs and expireds: Sources of listings you should not neglect.

Unless you are still in licensing school, you are probably breathing a sigh of relief because all these components are most likely familiar to you. There's no super-secret way to find clients that only Jedi-agents have access to. In fact, take another look at the list and think of all the spammy sales calls you receive. Those clever companies want you to pay them to prospect for you. *"Pay us to send pie recipe postcards to your farm." "Let us increase your web traffic." "Give us your money and we'll guarantee you FSBOs who will convert!"*

You can organically grow your business in all these areas, and all you need is your willingness to do the work in a systematic way that produces results over and over again. I'm about to show you the why and how of each component to create a clear path for your success.

One of the key principles you need to learn is how to balance these components in your weekly routine. Just like in the board game, if you only focus on one category you'll never complete your 'pie' and win the game. For example, if you only focus on open houses and don't have a database system in place, you'll lose track of some of your hard-earned leads. Sure, you may get a few closings from open houses, but without a database system in place, you lose the leverage you could have had with consistent communication with those open house leads.

A few years ago a competitor flagged my high-ranking website as spam and I lost several months of lead traffic. Ouch! Luckily, all the other components were still operating smoothly, so the sting was not nearly as bad as if I had only relied on web leads.

When I created that class, I could've drawn a circle in the middle labeled "Buyers/Sellers" and had the other five components on the outside with arrows pointing to the circle. This is how most agents run their businesses. They focus on the middle (working with buyers and sellers) and then run to the outside components—the prospecting components—when the buyers/sellers dry up and they need to grow again. That's no way to run a business! All components must be seen as equals on a constant growth cycle if you want to have a successful career free of periods without closings. Therefore, the Trivial Pursuit™ game piece is the perfect example. If you're only working with existing clients and not prospecting for new clients through the other five components, 5/6 of your business is a big empty spot.

In It to Win It!

First and foremost, you have to be in the game to win it. Whether you are newly licensed or have been an agent since agents had to rely on a printed book as their MLS system, you need to make sure you're treating it as your business. This means waking up every day ready to work.

The president of my company goodheartedly tells the story of an agent who keeps his suit ironed and ready to go everyday *just in case* someone calls him to see property. In my grade book, that agent gets an E for effort, but he'll never make an A. Buyers and sellers aren't calling random agents, saying, "Hello! Do you have your suit and tie ready to go? Yes? Then great, I'd like to see 123 Elm Street today at 4pm!" You must be in the trenches in real estate, going where your buyers and sellers are in order to make the sale. When you wake up, you need to have more than your outfit ready, you need to have a game plan in place to make your business *run*!

The truth of the matter is that if you do not have a success plan in motion that includes prospecting for new buyers and sellers, then you are not thriving in this business. You are merely a placeholder hoping to get lucky and catch some business. You'll never get out of your pajamas if you don't have a success plan, and it won't matter if your suit is ironed.

For example, some agents have a large sphere of influence (SOI) that makes it easy for them to 'catch' business. They think they can run their business solely on referrals, without needing to show up to other areas such as farming and open houses. While SOI is undeniably a huge part of a successful business, and you should be able to count on repeat business and referrals from your SOI throughout the years, you cannot expect to run on SOI alone and have a wildly successful career. Just think of the additional income potential when you include farming, open houses, and FSBOs/expireds! Build your database with those clients, and your SOI will grow at an exponential rate. Fully immerse yourself into each area of real estate to truly become a successful agent.

Just like a professional basketball player practices every day to become the best in his conference, or a Jenny Craig member counts calories (or points) at every meal, a real estate agent needs a daily practice in place to succeed. The moment an agent steps away, even if he has a generously-referring SOI, he is out of the game and his success will come to a halt. If you can commit yourself to your business everyday, then you are well on your way to achieving a well-rounded career.

Systems Create Balance

Why do so many agents fall prey to marketing scams that promise systems that will "change their careers forever"? Because the agent hears the word 'systems' and thinks *this must be it, the thing that will make everything easier for me!*

Systems can and should be terrific. They should provide a guideline for you to adhere to, and a method of tracking your success. If you have no system you are essentially flailing around, and that's no way to run a successful business. So when agents hear of a "New-Way-to-Get-Leads-System!" they jump on board . . . only to later find themselves unbalanced again and in need of closings so they can pay to stay in the system.

Follow the *right kind* of system, not a new, scammy-spammy one that over-promises, under-delivers and leaves you more unbalanced than before you began.

Your system that will succeed consists of the six components and a weekly schedule that keeps you in tune with those components and alerts you to deficiencies. In later chapters I'll show you how to dedicate time for each of these components every week. You'll learn to create a schedule you can look to each morning to make sure you are on track. Having a clear and focused game plan every day will prevent you from feeling frustrated, and from wondering if you are doing the right things to increase your income. When you have periods without closings, you can recheck your schedule and see if you had been neglecting a component.

No System	System
Wake up, hope someone calls me to sell their home, make some posts on my social media accounts and scan my friends' updates to see if anyone is moving soon, fall asleep feeling bored and unaccomplished.	Wake up, look at schedule that outlines activities to do in each of the six categories, stick to a strict plan to achieve the tasks at hand, go to sleep feeling accomplished.
Feel frustrated when my closings dry up. Wonder if this is the right business for me.	Identify weaknesses through analyzing my past schedule to see if I had been neglecting a component. Correct my schedule.

Knowing the areas of your business you need to focus on, and having a plan to work on them every day, is the kind of system that will lead you to be a thriving real estate agent. From years of speaking to frustrated agents, I know that not having this system in place is the number one reason for their negative feelings toward the business, and for their failure to succeed. As soon as they realize the scope of what their successful business entails and they have a clear system in place, they are on track to hit new income levels year after year.

In chapters 3 through 8, I'm going to show you each component in detail, supplemented by other tactics you can incorporate into the system, and then I'll tie them all together as your unified system for a successful real estate career. But first, some housekeeping. . . .

Chapter 2
Branding

You're about to hear a lot from me about building *your* business. To build a business, you must have a business to 'sell.' Unless you are working for a team that defines your role, <u>you are selling yourself</u>. You are telling buyers and sellers, "I am the real estate professional you should choose for your transaction." (And if you are on a team that defines what you can 'sell,' read on anyway; you'll want this information when you're ready to break free.)

How do you sell yourself? (Legally, of course!) You brand yourself. You give your audience a way to identify you. That identification should cling to you so tightly that any imagery of your branding automatically brings your name to mind.

Do you have a branding package in place? Here's how to tell if you don't:

- You're branding your company's logo (and you are not the head broker).
- You've hired someone to create a logo. It makes rare appearances, mostly on your business card.
- The logo you're using doesn't give people an emotional connection to you.

I loved my marketing classes in college. For group projects, we'd get a company assigned to us, such as Pepsi®, and we'd have to create an all-out marketing campaign for them (mock, of course, though I dreamed that Pepsi would hire me based on my A+ campaign I created for them in that class). Did the Pepsi logo just pop into your head? Could you recall the taste of Pepsi on your lips as you read the name? I haven't had a Pepsi in more than a decade, but I sure can recall the red and blue logo, the unique taste that can be conjured by its name, and the fizzy bubbles dancing on my tongue. That's branding in action.

Do you think my group mates and I veered much from those signature properties Pepsi will always be known for in our campaigns? No way! That would've resulted in a failing grade. Instead, we built upon the senses, the images, and the emotions the brand already evoked and found ways to make those values attractive to a target audience.

What senses do you as a real estate professional evoke? Taste won't really help you here unless you're famous in your community for baking apple pies for every closing. Be creative with the senses and how they translate to your business. Hearing = listening and trust. Sight = sold signs and houses. You can even correlate smell with real estate! A clean smell is a positive experience when thinking about real estate, which translates into using clean lines in your branding.

But we don't all want the same branding—a logo featuring a house drawn with clean lines and a sold sign in the front yard. Develop a brand that makes you stick out in your audience's mind so that when they think of real estate they think of YOU. (When you read the word 'Pepsi' earlier, you didn't think of

Orange Fanta!) Therefore, you need to define what makes *you* unique—your story—and how you do business.

My husband and I are partners in this business and we hired a marketing company to create our branding together. We each filled out an in-depth questionnaire, and the marketing company went to work defining who we are. Our branding reflects us: we are a middle-aged couple who lives in a specific part of town where we love entertaining clients and friends. The focus of our branding is the relationships we build with our clients.

How much money have you budgeted for a marketing company to create your brand? Despite my training in marketing, and that, as agents, we are marketing professionals, I felt it best to pay a marketing company thousands of dollars to create our brand. I wanted the vision an outside perspective could bring (although, looking back at the synopsis I described above, it was quite obvious what our branding should be). Sometimes that outside perspective is crucial to helping you define your brand. Agents can get caught up in copying what they think they should portray in their branding and miss the mark entirely, and fail to bring their unique personalities to the table.

There are companies that will create your campaign for less than what I spent, but make sure they understand the scope of the work needed (which I will describe next), and that they aren't simply creating a logo with a house and your initials.

Your Branding Package

When you meet with clients for the first time, what materials do you give to them? A company folder with mismatched letterhead inside? Nothing? Equip yourself with a complete branding package in place so that when you meet clients, or are prospecting for new ones, your material is consistent and professional. Your fully-customized package should include:

- A brochure written in third person that describes who you are and why you are in this business. This should not be a sales pitch, but rather a warm piece that makes your audience feel like they really know you. This is a key piece in connecting you to your brand in your audience's minds.
- Not-your-typical letterhead. You want truly branded letterhead that displays your branding and has a sidebar with your bio.
- Listing presentation material.
- Buyer's guide material.
- Banners for your website and social media accounts.
- Business cards, of course.
- Presentation folders.
- Extras could include envelopes, note cards and even stamps.

I spent several years as an agent without a complete, professional branding package, and I remember that the moment my material arrived, a huge weight was lifted off my shoulders. My branding package was the missing piece to feeling prepared and professional. Prospecting becomes a much smoother process for you when you have your branding package in place.

When I need to rush out to meet clients, I don't have to scramble and put together a presentation folder. More importantly, I know that the marketing pieces my audience sees (my clients and not-yet-clients) are so consistent that my brand becomes strong in their minds. The more pieces I send to my audience, the more likely they are to think of me when they think of real estate. I become the Pepsi of real estate to my audience (or the Coca-Cola® if you're a biased soda drinker). Branding accomplishes all of this—and not my broker's logo, or a generic outline of a house with my name written across it.

If you were to stop reading this book now you might suspect that I'm a marketing company trying to pitch my services to you. First, my artistic talents fall below the ability to make even the boring, generic house-and-name logo. Second, your branding is just your foundation for what is to come. I could have placed this chapter at the end of the book, but I wanted you to know about its importance up front so that you understand how to leverage the components of your business in the following chapters. If you follow all of the advice I am about to give you and use your broker's logo in your marketing materials, you can still do well in this business. But if you brand yourself so that your audience thinks of you when they think of real estate, you will have a powerful machine in place and be a top-producing agent.

Chapter 3
Buyers and Sellers

OVER THE LAST SEVERAL YEARS I've asked many agents who sat across the interview table from me, "Why did you get into real estate?" Some have said that they wanted to be in business for themselves. Others said they wanted to put their love of HGTV to monetary gain. But the most popular answer has always been, "Because I love helping people."

Most agents view working with buyers and sellers as their sole daily mission. Not only does working directly with buyers and sellers fulfill their desire to be in real estate, helping people, let's face it: working with buyers and sellers is the closest path to getting paid. This means the other components of their businesses, such as farming, open houses, and nurturing their database, take a backseat as mere *tactics* to attract more buyers and sellers. Putting all their efforts into each client and failing to prospect to grow their businesses results in periods without closings. When a buyer falls through or a listing doesn't sell, they are back at ground zero, waiting for another buyer or seller to come along so they can hop back on this bumpy cycle. It's no wonder so many agents burn out!

Jump off of that cycle and transform your business into a well-balanced, smooth running machine. In a machine, the many parts work together for a common goal. Your goal as an agent is **closings**, not just 'working with buyers and sellers.' Buyers and sellers are a means to your goal, just as the other components of your business are a means to getting more closings.

Before I get into detail about your work balance, I'm going to discuss exactly what I mean by working with buyers and sellers.

Buyers

Buyers are typically your first clients as a new agent. Many agents are blessed by loyal friends and family members who become their test run straight out of licensing school. Your sphere of influence (SOI) is generally the easiest place to find your first clients. This is why so many companies take on new agents! They realize that while the odds of an agent making it past their first year in real estate aren't the highest, at least they'll get a stab at business from that person's SOI (and hopefully find a superstar agent in the process, of course).

I still remember my first-ever buyer showing. On phone duty I intercepted a call to show duplexes in a part of town I had no real experience in. (Actually, I had no experience in any parts of town at this time!) Eager and excited to have this opportunity, I did all the research I could in the small timeframe before my showing, and jumped in my car the minute phone duty was over to meet this sweet out-of-state family who had dreams of buying an investment property in Austin. I certainly did not want to shoot down their hopes and dreams by asking for proof that they could purchase. I mean, who was *I*, a newbie agent, to judge? (Ha!) Over the next week I abandoned dinners, dropped plans, and drove to all corners of my city to show this family every possible duplex, triplex and fourplex available. Then I got the call, "Shannon, sorry we won't be able to buy a duplex, we can't get a loan because we don't have citizenship and we don't have enough money without a loan."

Was I sad? A little—especially when I thought of the way I'd hurriedly left my fiancée in the middle of dinner one night to show a property to this family. But really, I was glad for the experience they gave me. My feet—well, maybe just my toes—were wet and I had gained the confidence I needed when a close friend mentioned over drinks that he'd like to buy some investment properties. He'd heard me discussing showing the duplexes and no longer saw me as an agent straight out of licensing school, but instead as an agent with some experience under her belt. Even if there was no money in my bank account to make me feel experienced, it was experience enough to an outsider's eyes. Very soon after, I had multiple buy and list transactions with that friend.

You may relate to my story, or maybe you received your first buyer from an open house or a networking group. Some new agents have enough capital coming into the business to advertise themselves heavily, whether through print media (such as magazines or billboards) or online, and this is how they receive their first buyers.

Buyers can be repeat customers, turning into sellers along the way, and are great referral sources. But you must actively look for new buyers to fill the gaps while you wait for them to buy again. This is why the other areas of your business are equally important.

Anatomy of Working with Buyers

1. Agent meets buyer.

2. Buyer asks to see anywhere from 1 to 100 homes.

3. Agent takes buyer to see anywhere from 1 to 400 homes.

4. Agent helps buyer write offer on a property.

5. Agent helps buyer write offer on another property because the first offer fell through.

6. Repeat steps 2-5 as necessary.

7. Agent assists buyer throughout the buying process once under contract, including the loan process, inspections, repair requests, negotiations, and vendor recommendations (home warranty, insurance, contractors).

8. Agent works to make sure all terms of contract are met, and that all necessary title documents are sent to the buyer in a timely manner.

9. Buyer does final walk-through with agent. Agent talks them through their cold feet and manages third parties (such as in-laws).

10. Agent and buyer hug over the closing table. Agent leaves with commission check in hand.

That is the anatomy of working with buyers in a nutshell. The process can be physically and emotionally grueling. 'Rewarding' is another term I like to call it. Many times, after a closing, my clients and I go through withdrawal pangs. You become such a large part of your buyers' lives during the process, and once the closing occurs you begin to miss each other. (Of course, this is true only if the transaction went well!) This is when one of the other components of your business steps in: your database. Once you have a closed buyer, they are moved to your database and through your consistent nurturing of your database, the withdrawal becomes less severe because you stay in touch.

In the list above, you didn't see the step where working with one buyer turns into a year's worth of closings, did you? Sure, if your buyer is a wealthy investor who plans to load up their portfolio this year, you're in luck—and a buyer can single-handedly give you a year's worth of referrals if they have an outstanding SOI themselves. But in order to get more buyers, prospecting through the other components of your business is necessary. Therefore, working with buyers—this means the home showings, the negotiations and the offer-writing—needs to become only a portion of your day, not your entire day's work.

Sellers

As mentioned above, new agents typically find buyer-clients first, and that's because sellers tend to expect more experience from their agents. I believe it's equally important to have a good agent on either side of the equation, but somehow buyers tend to be more lax about their agent's experience than sellers. This is most likely due to the interview process when homeowners begin the list process. I have certainly experienced competitive buyer interviews that felt like I was applying for a position at a Fortune

500 company, but the majority of buyer interviews go like this: "Hi! Can you show me this property today at 6pm?"

Sellers, on the other hand, approach a real estate transaction with more apprehension. They worry about and want to compare commission negotiation, marketing plans, showing schedules, prepping the home to sell and, most importantly to them, how much money they can make. To find the agent who can give them the perfect combination of all these elements, they interview the agent from the biggest company nearby, the agent who always leaves flags on their driveway for the 4th of July, the agent they see advertised in the weekly paper, the agent their friend used, and their third cousin who is a part-time agent.

My first listing was with a previous buyer-client of mine. He was one of the toughest clients I had ever worked with, and I contemplated firing him after I caught wind of him calling the listing agent (we were buy-side at the time) and posing as a broker in order to pry information out of him! I begrudgingly kept him in my database, and through my database work I maintained a relationship with him. He refused to list with anyone but me.

Your raving fans will be some of your best clients, so make sure you keep in touch with them long after the closing table. In fact, amp up your contact with them three to seven years after their purchase, because these are the years people are most likely to sell again.

Anatomy of Working with Sellers

1. Agent is interviewed by seller and is usually competing against several other agents.
2. Seller decides which agent to hire.
3. Agent helps seller prepare home for sale.
4. Agent lists and markets home for sale.
5. Agent puts home on broker tour.
6. Agent loses sleep each day that passes without an offer.
7. Agent negotiates offer(s).
8. Agent handles sellers' emotions throughout offer negotiations and any repair negotiations.
9. Agent talks seller off the ledge when they announce they no longer want to move, despite the fact they are supposed to close on the home they are buying in two days and cannot back out of either contract without default.
10. Agent and seller hug at closing table. Agent walks away with commission check.

If the experience was good for the seller, they will be a good referral source for you. If they are staying in your market area, they can be repeat clients for you. However, once that listing closes, you will be left scrambling to find your next sale unless you have a system in place to constantly replenish your active client base.

An agent once told me that he couldn't wait to get his first listing, because that would mean he would forever get more listings on that same street. He truly thought "For Sale" signs multiplied overnight.

You *can* leverage one listing into multiple listings and long-term staying power in a neighborhood if you diligently work the other five components, especially farming and open houses. If you spend each day immersed in the activities listed in the anatomy above, and ignore the other components, your sign will disappear from the neighborhood as soon as your listing sells and your momentum to multiply that sign will be lost.

Balancing Clients with Prospecting

Let this sink in: if you are only working with buyers and sellers—showing homes, going on listing appointments and marketing your listings—you will run out of buyers and sellers to work with. This is why you must treat the other components of your business with as much diligence as you give to your buyers and sellers. You must continually prospect for new buyers and sellers so that you always have more closings lined up. Sure, your current clients will refer people to you occasionally, if you gave them great service, but without prospecting for new buyers and sellers your closings will dry up.

Spend time in all areas of your business, not just showing and marketing homes for your buyers and sellers. You should drop your time spent in this area from 100% to somewhere in the 50% range to free up more time to attract new clients and have a steady stream of closings in your future.

Wait! Before you slam this book shut and throw it across the room in horror (or delete it from your online app), let me explain. I know you're thinking, "But, Shannon! I spend day and night showing homes and going on listing appointments. Now you're telling me that should only be 50% of my time?! You're a crazy lady who must think the day has 40 hours in it! If I cut down on my time spent with clients, I won't have *any* closings!"

I'm sure you've heard the phrase 'work smarter, not harder.' Your schedule needs to be working smart for you. Do you have clients who want to see 1,000 homes before making an offer? Those clients need to be put on a shorter leash so they can make a decision, and this is good for them and good for you. Dictate to them your available time and make them respect your parameters. Show them you're looking out for their best interests while still showing them the houses you know fit their criteria best, and they will be loyal to you. (In Chapter 10, Implementation, I'll show you how to take control of your schedule and empower you to set limits with your clients.) Your goal is to examine when you should be working with buyers and sellers and how you can make time for creating new business for yourself. New business is critical to growing your business.

I'd also like to add that if you are spending most of your day showing properties or working on listings, it is time to consider hiring an assistant who can help you with the menial tasks such as scheduling showings and marketing tasks. This will free up more of your time. Agents who once feared letting go of control to an assistant and the required financial outlay find themselves in new, higher income brackets once they make the leap, hire an assistant, and gain more time to grow their business.

If you work for a team or brokerage that gives you leads, consider those leads as bonuses. Don't rely on your broker to provide your next lead. Actively look for your next client as if the lead well is going to dry up tomorrow. Because guess what? It could. I've seen way too many agents turn around after a closing and hold their hands out, saying, "Gimme." Those agents would starve if the next lead wasn't handed to them. They are barely surviving. Do you want to survive or *thrive* in this business?

Benjamin Franklin said, "If you fail to plan, you are planning to fail." No words could ring truer in real estate. Successful agents plan out their weeks and know how to predict their closings because they have a system in place to ensure they do not fail. Unsuccessful agents run without a plan and hope to get lucky and have business handed to them. They are left feeling tired and frustrated when months go by without a closing.

Two of my favorite real estate books are Michael Maher's *The Seven Levels of Communication* and *The Miracle Morning for Real Estate Agents*, which Maher co-authored with Hal Elrod, Jay Kinder and Michael Reese. In those two books, the success themes are the power of time-blocking your schedule and waking up every morning with intention. If Benjamin Franklin were still around, he'd give those authors a round of applause because they have mastered planning to succeed.

In Chapter 10 I will discuss how your schedule should combine and designate time for all the components of your business, but for now let's stick with the focus of this chapter: buyers and sellers.

Each Monday, you should have a general idea of which buyers and sellers you are working with that week. Of course, the phone can ring at any moment with a showing request or listing appointment, but first let's address the clients you already know you are working with. Monday morning is an ideal time to organize your schedule for the week, since it is after your busy weekend, but if another day works better for you, change to that day. Get your worksheet and *pencil* ready. (Visit www. ShannonEnsor.com/realestatemachine/resources/ to find your downloadable worksheet.)

First, think about your buyers. They tend to be on the needier side of the spectrum compared to sellers; you can show a buyer dozens of homes in one week, but you're only selling one house at a time per seller (except in investor situations of course, but for this exercise we'll view our sellers in terms of addresses, not the client). What do you know about your buyers' schedules? Who is in town only for the weekend, and who has strict work hours? Make a list, beginning with your clients who are not yet under contract. Place them at the top of your list because they are the most time-sensitive. Are they getting out-bid in a red-hot market where there is low inventory, or are they searching in a rural area where listings don't come along very often? Rank them based on this information. You wouldn't want to be unavailable to show a buyer a home that just went live on the MLS system in a multiple-offer market because you had to hang out at another buyer's inspection, would you? I sure hope not! You're setting yourself up for not only missing the chance to win that property, but you may lose your client in the process.

On your calendar, shade the times of day that each client has available to view homes. You can get fancy and use different colors for each client (or type of client), or you can simply write their names in each spot. You may have clients who have yet to nail down showing times with you and their available times overlap with other clients, and this is okay. You are going for a general idea of your schedule at this point so you can see what you are working with and how to best tailor your schedule.

Now you ask, "What about my clients who seem to want to see homes 24/7 and have no other life right now?" Put those clients on your list, but do not yet designate a time for them. We're going to narrow the times on the chart from when your clients *expect you* to be available to when you will *actually* be available.

Move on to your buyers who are under contract. Are you in mid-negotiations with a buyer? Have you already scheduled inspections, final walk-throughs, closings, or other times where you need to be present this week? Items such as final walk-throughs can be more critical than hanging around an inspection, so prioritize those appointments on your calendar.

Agents gasp when I announce that I don't go to every single one of my closings. I don't even attend most of my buyers' inspections. Why? Because I have to prioritize my schedule and be where I know my time is best spent. I cannot physically or legally inspect a property, so really, I am just around for entertainment purposes during inspections. The most important time of the inspection is the last 20 minutes when the inspector typically prefers to go over any deficiencies with the buyer. Even then I prefer not to be present so I can force the buyer to digest the information given to them by the inspector without putting myself in hot water by accidentally offering opinion. For example, and thank goodness this is not a personal example, if you say at an inspection, "Oh, that leaky faucet is no big deal, you can fix that easily with a new one after closing," you are setting yourself up for a lawsuit when it turns out that faucet was an indication of a larger problem, and your client felt as though you advised them to ignore it!

Spend your time wisely and appropriately.

I feel the same way about closings. If I've scoured the closing statement for mistakes before the closing and all seems to be moving along fine, I leave the closing process to the escrow agents if I have another appointment that needs my actual attention. Remember, your clients are big boys and girls and as long as you've done your duties to the fullest for them, stop the excessive hand-holding and put your time and attention into running your business.

This is when agents gasp even louder! "I really know you're crazy now, Shannon! My clients gush and gush about me because I attended their inspections and closings. My attendance is a must!"

If you do a good job for your clients, regardless of whether you show up to appointments where your presence is merely for moral support, they will sing your praises. Early in my career a client asked me at a closing, "What are you doing here? Shouldn't you be out working?" He was a savvy client and knew my presence wasn't necessary.

Still shaking your head and can't possibly imagine prioritizing something else over a closing? Remember, you can do something special with your client before or after the closing. Give them your thank you note and gift in a different scenario where you aren't also picking up a paycheck. Separate the two concepts and you will show deeper gratitude to your client—and gain greater control of your schedule.

Let's go back to your weekly calendar. Now that you have a

good idea of times you *should* allocate for your buyers, move on to your sellers. Do you have any listing appointments set up? Schedule them in pen. Does this create a buyer conflict? If it's a buyer who has a flexible schedule, there is no conflict. You are simply no longer available to that buyer during your listing appointment. If the listing appointment conflicts with the only time the buyer has available because they're flying in and out in that same day, or some other scenario, then you need to work it out now—who can you move? Your solution may be to refer one of the two out to another agent.

Next, schedule marketing time for your listings in pencil. How many listings do you currently have? Do you have a new-to-market listing that will require several hours on one day so that you can upload into the MLS, make flyers, and blast the virtual tour out to other agents and your social media? Do you have an assistant who handles any of those items for you? For your older listings, schedule twenty minutes per listing to revitalize each one's marketing plan. If you have a property tour scheduled, be sure to add that in as well.

Is your entire week now shaded and labeled with appointments? It's time to start chopping out time for prospecting. I'm going to go over the time frames for those in the following chapters, but for now, you *need* to develop the habit of seeing where your buyers and sellers need you and where they want you and learn how to effectively schedule them so that your time isn't taken over by them. This leaves you with room to grow your business. By planning out your week, and designating when you should meet with your buyers and sellers and when you should be doing other activities to grow your business, you will have a successful plan in place that never leaves you feeling frustrated.

I'd like to tackle an objection I can hear coming my way before this chapter ends, because I've heard it before. "But working with buyers and sellers is how I grow my business. I give them exceptional service and then they send me referrals and give me repeat business. I certainly won't stop going to their closings— that's where I give them their gorgeous closing gift and we all sing Kumbaya around the closing table!" I'm here to tell you: **you can create exceptional service throughout the entire buying and selling process *and* maintain a schedule that allows you to grow your business.** Your clients will sing your praises even if you are not present for the entire three-hour inspection, as long as you negotiate their repairs like a champion. It is essential that you give exceptional service so that you receive referrals AND have time to grow your business. You can't do one and not the other and thrive in this business.

Chapter 4
Database

CREATING, DEVELOPING, AND MAINTAINING your database is one of the most crucial elements of your business, yet the one agents tend to struggle with the most. Causes of struggle include lack of organizational skills, laziness, the perception of being too busy to do the work, and getting tangled up in deciding on a database management product without follow-through. If any of these struggles apply to you, I'm going to help you get through them. If you already have a great database system in place, you'll benefit from learning strategies to grow your database and use it to work smarter, not harder.

Your database is made up of everyone you know—your SOI (sphere of influence), the people you are meeting through the other components of your business (such as open house leads and Internet leads), and the people you meet through networking.

Because your database is filled with people who either know and like you already or have opted-in to be on your list, it is one of your easiest places to turn to for business. You don't have to cold-call your database. Your database is a pool of people who are more likely to purchase or sell real estate through you than a stranger—as long as they can remember that you are an active agent!

Are you on a team that hands leads to you? Are you thinking, "Why worry about a database? I'll just work the leads that come in. Next please!"? You may be rocking and rolling, have plenty of closings lined up, and life seems good. Until it's not. If you aren't working to build your business, you won't have a business to fall back on when your team leader or broker decides to go another route, or their leads dry up.

Or maybe you're a solo agent who hasn't had to worry about an efficient database system up to this point. Referrals seem to easily fall in your lap and clients make sure to stay in touch with you. Until they don't. Remember, as an agent you are building your empire. A long, successful career requires more than jumping from closing to closing; it is about building a sustainable business that will allow you to thrive and grow exponentially. Your database is your biggest sweet spot when it comes to growing your business. You should never become too busy to nurture and grow something that has the potential to propel your career over and over again.

When I first moved to Austin, Texas, I knew one person besides my fiancée. My friends and family were three hours away in the Dallas/Fort Worth area, though many high school friends had moved away for college, just as I had. I had just left behind my sphere of influence in Arizona, where I had spent most of my college days and the years following. And somehow I got the crazy idea to become a real estate agent! So, with only one local person in my database, I got to work.

If I can start out in this business only knowing one person in my city and become a top-producing agent in only five years, I know you can too. You're just going to need the same mindset I had: commitment to growing and nurturing your database every. single. day.

Zero Tolerance Zone

I know you aren't surprised to read "work your database." This is the first thing every agent learns. Yet it never fails that this is one of the biggest weak spots for agents. When it comes to your database, you need to commit 100%. Excuses are unacceptable. Develop zero tolerance for any slack whatsoever in maintaining your database.

Maintaining any less than 100% of your database will leave you feeling frustrated, with that feeling of "I know I need to be doing *something* right now...," and you become vulnerable to marketing systems that want you to pay them to manage your database. Some systems are fantastic, but I warn against wasting money on the new hot product of the moment as a solution to your problem. Be wise where you spend your dollars. Find a system and stick to it 100%.

A database can cost you as little as $0 if you already have software like Excel on your computer; it can be that simple! I have two running Excel sheets: "Database—Emails" and "Database—Home Addresses." Everyone I know is entered into my email list, but the home address list is saved for those I'll receive greater ROI (return on investment) from. I'll explain ROI in a moment.

I also suggest you have some kind of CRM (customer relationship management) in place so you can create groups and tag your contacts. In this way you can identify the golfers, for example, so you can send them pieces of information on golf course homes. Or you can have a group labeled, "People I Met at Open Houses." A CRM makes your life easier when you email your monthly newsletter, because it provides statistics on email open rates and usually has built-in features that keep you FTC complaint. Most CRMs allow you to easily import and export your database to Excel, so you can have everything in one central location. A free CRM came with the web tool I use to generate leads (my IDX system).

Once you have your system, upload **everyone** you know into it. Every person you know on this planet, whether they live in your city or not, can be a referral source for you, so they need to be a part of your database. This will allow you to consistently send them something that identifies you as your region's go-to agent. All the buyers and sellers from the previous chapter should be in your database.

Your surprise database group: other agents. You especially want to add agents from other cities who have referred business in the past, or to whom you have referred business. And be sure to include other agents in your area who know and like you— you never know how long their real estate career will last, or if they will move out of your area, and they can become a source of referrals for you one day. Along these lines, add other people you do business with such as title company reps, lenders, insurance agents, even your dry cleaner.

Commit right now to tackling your database. Don't let another week pass without uploading everyone you know into your database. You will feel accomplished and the nagging presence of

I know I'm not doing everything I need to be doing will disperse. Get a system you relate to, whether it is the Excel spreadsheet or a CRM system, and set aside a full day to do nothing but enter everyone you know into your database. Imagine the weight that will fall off your shoulders when you've compiled everyone neatly into a system. No more scraps of paper tucked away in office drawers, or stacks of business cards piling up. Your productivity levels will skyrocket from this exercise alone. Next, set aside time **every single day** to add to your database so that you never fall behind again.

Updating your database needs to be a habit, just like brushing your teeth before bed. Every night, think about each new person you met that day and who you've collected information from, and enter them into your database. From a business card you received at a networking event to the Internet lead that only gave you his email address and first name, enter everyone into your database by the end of every day so that you can start the next day with a completed database. To create a habit of doing this, set an alarm in your phone to alert you one hour before your typical bedtime: "Time to update my database!" Set the alarm to go off every day for the next 30 days, which is arguably the length of time needed to form a habit. If at the end of the 30 days you find that you skipped days, you might consider a different time of day that would work better for you. Perhaps your evenings are frazzled because you have young children, and that time of day is unreliable. Maybe updating your database each morning with the previous day's contacts will work better for you, so set a new alarm for 30 days, and keep at it until updating your database becomes second nature to you. The point is that it needs to be a reliable daily habit.

This daily exercise of thinking who you met may jog your memory, and will show you that you meet more new people each day than you realize. This is why it is so important to do a **daily** recap and add everyone you can think of. If you let days slip by, you will forget meetings that seemed minor. If you add them daily, those meetings will still seem fresh and relevant—and your database will grow stronger.

As you're reading this book you're visualizing a clear track to your success. You're getting fired up! But what happens when you put the book down? Are you going to walk over to your computer and research CRM companies? There are so many your head will be spinning before you know it. Then what? You get overwhelmed, shelve the idea for now, and months go by and no one in your database hears from you. Sales opportunities are lost. You know you need to do something about your database, but blocking it out of your mind just seems so much easier right now. Let's end that cycle. Talk to your broker or find a Facebook group where real estate professionals collaborate about products they like. Find a system and put your database into action. *Today.*

Outside of your CRM and your schedule, you don't need a fancy system in place to connect with your database. Be genuine with your database. "Database"—what a cold-sounding word we use to describe some of our biggest cheerleaders. Let that coldness and jargon stay between us during our technical discussions about real estate, and connect with your database with familiar warmth and genuineness. Comb through your database and define the special connection you have with each person in it.

Early in my real estate career I met a woman at an open house who seemed to be doing her best to dodge me. In the short time

I had to make an initial connection with her, I learned that she was from upstate New York. I've never even been to New York (I know, I can't believe I am admitting that to you right now!). However, another friend of mine was also from upstate NY, so I made that slight connection with my guest. "Oh, I have a friend from upstate, too." She walked out the door and I beat myself up. *Another open house guest that won't turn into a sale.* But I'm persistent and kept her in my database anyway. One day I called her—I had nothing to lose, right? I introduced myself, "Hi, this is Shannon. We met at an open house a couple of weeks ago—" She cut me off, "I remember! You have the friend from upstate! I've been meaning to call you. I need an agent, are you available to show me some homes this weekend?" Long story short, she's bought two homes and sold one through me . . . so far.

Make a connection with the people you meet, no matter how seemingly insignificant it seems to you in that moment. This makes you seem real to the people in your database. You have to feel real to them before you can build rapport and earn their business—and their repeat business. This business isn't about churn and burn, or the latest technology; it's about connecting with people and creating those lasting relationships. And it's about working smarter by connecting with your database.

Commit to following through with people in your database by scheduling blocks of time each week. For example, set aside 9am-10am, Monday - Friday for database contact. You will soon find that the hours you spend prospecting within your database are your most enjoyable and fulfilling moments each week.

Nurture vs. Nature

Once your system is in place, meaning everyone you know is in your database and it has become second nature to add people daily, you must nurture your database. Your database is not a show pony. It won't do tricks for you unless you are doing something with it to make it work for you. There is great debate over how often you should contact your database. You'll hear mentors suggest anywhere from eight times a year to 33. To nurture your database, I suggest the following:

- Monthly email newsletter. If you have a CRM system in place, this may be a free tactic for you—bonus! This means 12 times a year your database should expect to receive an email newsletter from you. Schedule this in your calendar now. Don't let one month go by without your database at least receiving this (often free) contact. I urge you to make the newsletter somewhat personal; generic newsletter services reek of salesy-cheesiness that repulse your audience rather than entice them to contact you.

  I'm pretty fortunate. At my brokerage we have an administrative assistant who puts together our monthly newsletters with each agent's personal branding. She does the legwork to find information relevant to people's lives for that particular month and sends out a helpful email. The key words are <u>relevant</u> and <u>helpful</u>. Because of this, *every* time a newsletter goes out, I receive

responses from my database, and I know that if I don't
hear from some of my database, that's okay because
at least my name and branding is staying in front of
them on a monthly basis. After each newsletter goes
out, I receive referrals or a call to help someone
with their purchase/sale. Get this system into place
for your database *this* month and see the results in
action. (Total = 12)

- Monthly postcard. Not only should you 'touch' your
  database once a month electronically, you should also
  send them something that they can hold in their hands.
  Postcards are effective because they are high impact
  design-wise and don't require your recipient to open
  an envelope to receive your impression. At my
  company, a roundtable of agents meets each year and
  decides on postcard topics for the next year that will
  encourage interaction from our databases. Our office
  assistant creates the postcard, brands them uniquely
  to each agent, and sends them to our databases.
  If your company does not do this, find a system that
  works for you. The most important elements are
  consistency, personal branding, and interaction. When
  your database gets accustomed to receiving your
  postcards each month, they will begin to look forward
  to the next one—and believe me, they will notice if
  you forget to send it! There is a difference between a
  postcard that stimulates a response from your audience
  and one that falls dead. If you send out a
  "Happy Halloween" postcard in October, it's

going straight to the trash. Interaction occurs when your postcard instead encourages them to visit your Facebook page to enter your pumpkin decorating contest. (Total = 12)

- Phone call once a year, minimum. Designate a segment of your database to call each month—this is easily done by last names. (January: last names that begin with A-B, February: C-D, and so on.) Your goal in this conversation is not to ask them to buy or sell a home, but to *connect* with them. Ask them about their lives. Show that you care by mentioning things that are specific to them. Focus the conversation on them. Do not focus the conversation on you or your achievements, be negative under any circumstance, or only pretend to hear what they are saying. Truly listen to them and ask this one important question: "How can I help you?" Perhaps someone mentions her child is having a hard time in school, giving you the opportunity to refer her to some tutors. Find ways you can make an impact in the lives of the people in your database and they will make an impact on your income in return. For some, this phone call will be an invitation to meet for face-to-face time, which we will discuss in a bit. (Total = 1/per database member; divided up throughout the year.)
- At least three more times a year, repeat the types of contact listed above on special occasions. Whatever seems most appropriate to you, call/email/send a handwritten card to your database on their birthdays, major holidays like Christmas, and their anniversary

date (whether you use the anniversary of buying their home, of working with you, or of their wedding). I can still recall the name of our agent when I was 6 years old because every year, like clockwork, we received birthday and anniversary cards from her. Decades later, I still associate her with real estate in my hometown (despite my not living there for two decades). You want that kind of impact on your database. (Total = at least 3.)

- Random contacts throughout the year. I will describe this in greater depth when we get to the social media chapter, but a majority of your database should be connected with you in some other way so that you have opportunities to be in front of them repeatedly throughout the year. For instance, meeting with select members of your database over coffee or lunch.

(Total = at least 1, although this is truly unlimited.)

This represents a sum total of at least 29 times a year you should be in front of your database. With 52 weeks in a year, this means two weeks shouldn't go by without your database hearing from you in some form.

Remember Chapter 2, on personal branding? Not only does your branding package make you look and feel more prepared and professional when you work with buyers and sellers, it makes an impact with your database. Consistent personal branding throughout your postcards and newsletters is the one-two combination you hit your database with each month: professionalism and 'stickability.' Sometimes it is the people who know you best that need to be assured of your professionalism, and personal branding delivers that high impact professionalism.

For the members of your database who know you less, consistent branding is what helps you stick in their minds as the go-to agent.

If you don't have an effectively running database that you are constantly nurturing and growing, you are going to fail in this business. You may *get by*, but you won't have a happy, fulfilling career, and to me that's worse than failing. Make it a priority to schedule time for your database each week. Have a weekly, monthly and yearly plan in place for when you are going to contact each person in your database—and stick to it! Nothing stings more than when someone in your database uses another agent. Prevent that from happening through consistently staying in front of your database.

Categorize Your Database for Highest ROI

After you've loaded everyone into your database, and you have a system in place to nurture them at least 29 times a year, it is time to categorize or rank each member. Set a system that makes sense to you—whether it's a grade system (A-team, B-team, etc.) or whether you categorize by color (red for red-hot buyers/ sellers, green for people who are active referral sources, yellow for past clients, blue for people you haven't had much contact with yet), make it a system that you understand and can easily decipher who goes in each category.

Everyone in your database, regardless of rank, should receive a monthly email newsletter from you, especially if it's free for you to send. Since postcards cost you money each month, you will want to be more selective with who receives those. Your database can be well over 1,000 emails, but you may only want to send to 250 home addresses each month. (And 250 is the ideal minimum.) This means your cousin in another state who you've never done business with, and who has yet to send a referral, is probably not an ideal candidate for your postcard. She'd fall into your C-team, or blue category. Categorization helps you decide who is postcard-worthy so your money is best spent.

When you call your database each month to say hi and ask if there is anything you can help them with, ask your top-tier people out for lunch or coffee. These are the people you are most familiar with, you've done business with, and/or they have referred business to you. They deserve some face time with you. If phone calls give you knots in your stomach, place your top-tiered people first on your call list so you get in the groove with the more pleasant and natural conversations. There's no easier opening than, "Hey, Jim! Are you free next week to grab some coffee?" This will help loosen those knots for the less familiar conversations, like, "Hello (person I met at an open house last month), how has your new job been going?" or "Hello (local financial advisor), how can I help you in your business?"

When your database is in place and you are actively growing and nurturing it, you have a well-run machine in place that takes out the 'Where am I going, what am I doing?' frustration. Your database also allows you to track how fast or slow your business is growing so you can fine-tune your goals. And this leads me to a frequently asked question: "How many people should I add to my database each day/week/month/year?" Some systems teach you to aim for five people a day, or to put 10 pennies in your pocket and move a penny to the opposite pocket every time you speak to someone new. If those systems work for you, great. But in the following chapters I'm going to show you ways to add to your database naturally, and through integrating the other components of your business. Each day's schedule will be different, and the possibilities to add to your database will vary from day to day. I suggest focusing more on growing your business purposely through each component, rather than forcing yourself to meet five random strangers each day. Through this method you'll find that your database connections will be more meaningful and productive to you.

Chapter 5
Internet and Social Media

I'M GOING TO ASSUME THAT YOU have a website and at least one social media account, whether it is Facebook, Twitter, LinkedIn, Instagram, or even Pinterest. Just in case you don't: Go! Go now and get one!

Your target market (buyers and sellers) is online and you need to be there, too. Help them remember that you are an agent by showing up where they are (which is online, checking their Facebook accounts). If they cannot remember that you are an agent, they will use another agent to help them with their next real estate transaction. Plus, sellers will expect you to market their listings online. Bottom line: There is no excuse not to be online.

Being online contributes to your well-rounded, successful career. Let's start by looking at the three online must-dos:

- Have the tools in place.
- Create content within your tools.
- Connect with your audience through your content and through their content.

The Right Tools

Growing your business online means you need to have the following in place:

- A personal website with a custom IDX and a blogging platform (WordPress is the most popular).

- Social media, which includes Facebook (a personal page and a business page), Instagram, Pinterest, YouTube, LinkedIn, Twitter . . . the list goes on. You pick which one(s) suit you best, and that you know you will actually use.

Build a Lead-Generating Website. Your custom IDX allows people to perform home searches on your site from the listing data that feeds from your affiliated MLS system. More importantly, it gives you lead capture capability. If you're using your company's IDX system and the leads are not going directly to you, you do not have a custom IDX solution and you need to get one right away. Don't give away your hard-earned traffic! Make sure your web leads come to YOU, not your company. This lead capture system is your #1 way to turn cold Internet leads into ready-to-go buyers and sellers.

You must also have a CRM or database management system in place so that you can keep in front of any slow-to-move Internet leads. An agent in my office closed an Internet lead that she had consistently stayed in front of through drip emails for more than two years! This is a prime example of moving leads into your database as prospects, and then later into the buyer/ seller category.

I know many agents who have done the above: they have their WordPress website, their custom IDX and a few pages on buying and selling, and a bio page. However, they never get any leads. Why not? Because they do not have any *traffic* going to their sites.

There are two ways to get traffic to your site: paid and organic. Paid traffic comes through ads you can run (paying the search engines for top placement), and organic traffic occurs when a lead lands on your site via a search engine, typically because you've done the work to rank high in the search engines. Unless you are from a small town with only a few agents, none of whom are tech-savvy, it is a battle to organically rank on page one of any search engine. The major outlets, like Realtor.com, Zillow and Redfin, dominate the top positions for home searches, and then you compete with every other agent from your board for the remaining spots on the coveted first page space. Not many buyers are willing to go past page one to do a home search; they have no need to, because they can always find what they need on the first page.

You can pay the major search engines for page one rank, or you can increase your organic traffic through content, which I'll discuss next. Another way to boost traffic to your website and blog—and more importantly, boost your leads—is to make sure you utilize widgets on your site to feed in your posts from your social media accounts. Allow technology, via a widget, to feed fresh content into your site, showing the big guys like Google, Yahoo and Bing that your site is fresh and relevant. I love how technology helps us to work smarter, don't you? If technology is a little foreign to you, there are plenty of books and websites that will help you learn the jargon and guide you through setting up a website with widgets.

Social Media Presence. Whether you are on Twitter, Facebook, LinkedIn, Instagram, Pinterest or one of the many others sites (it seems like new ones pop up every day!) the point is to *be there*! Personally, I'm a huge Facebook fan, I dabble in LinkedIn, and use Twitter simply to promote blog links and events. Having a social media presence:

- allows you to connect to your SOI and stay on top of what is going on in their lives;
- allows you to connect to new people you meet, whether personally or in a business context;
- provides an outlet for you to advertise listings, open houses and blog posts; and
- boosts your credibility through likes/followers.

Almost all the sites I've mentioned will allow you to personalize a banner or background image. Therefore, your branding should be displayed on your website, Facebook business page, Twitter, LinkedIn and YouTube—and any others that allow personalization. Consistent branding makes you look professional and helps you remain memorable in your audience's minds.

Set up your sites and accounts and link as many together as possible, and be sure they are branded to you. Once you have this part of your machine running, it's time to keep it well-oiled.

Content is King

This is the part where agents tend to get overwhelmed. *Set up my website and Facebook business page, sure! That was easy. Oh, now I have to keep up with them? UGH!*

A website without unique content is simply an online business card—meaning it lacks content that can organically drive traffic to the site, or a reason for traffic to stay on the site once they've found it. Social media accounts that go unused are dead and have no chance of getting any attention; and for savvy customers, an inactive account suggests that you are no longer in business. Regular, unique content is critical for search engine optimization and for presence in front of your audience.

While the chances are slim that you'll rank for property addresses (unless they're your own listings and you've done your work to get your marketing to show up in the search engines under your listing addresses), you can begin to rank for neighborhoods through blog posts. Yes, the major outlets have figured this out too, and most have neighborhood pages that rule over the first page, but there is still room for us little guys because of the wonderful world of blogging.

When a buyer searches for the intimate details of a neighborhood, they go past the non-local websites and dive into locally-written blogs. They want to know what it's like to live in the neighborhood they are considering. They want the up close and personal, and this is where you, the local agent with experience in the communities you are working, can *thrive*.

Give your personal accounts of neighborhoods in which you have listings, have represented buyers (or simply toured with buyers), that you farm, and that you do open houses in. Through those types of blog posts you will gain traction, organically rise up in the search engine ranks, and start to obtain buyer and seller leads. Blog posts also give you credibility; buyers and sellers will come to you to be represented because they want someone with neighborhood experience and credibility on their side.

If you're groaning because you'd rather hear nails scratch across a chalkboard than write a blog post, I have good news for you. Your posts only need to contain two things: your personality, and a call to action (CTA).

First, you need personality so that your readers can connect to *you*. Thinking of chalkboards again? Don't overthink your posts. Write as if you were talking to your friend about the neighborhood. Avoid sounding like an encyclopedia entry.

I once had an agent tell me she worked all day on her neighborhood blog post and she still couldn't come up with anything worth posting. It was torture for her. I learned she was trying to write an encyclopedia entry! Of course that is too hard; it wasn't natural for her to write that way. And if she felt it was bad, you know her readers would feel the same way. I told her to go home, have a glass of wine, and try again as if she were telling her friend about her neighborhood—and to *stop* writing after an hour. She soon turned in an excellent post and said it was hard to stop writing, and she was inspired to write more posts. The result? She produced something that people could *connect* to.

A year later, I can search her neighborhood name and still find her blog post on the first page of the results. More importantly, the CTA at the end of the post turns her reader connections into leads. Without a CTA at the end of your posts, your reader may move on to another site. When that happens, you've lost them— sometimes forever. CTAs are critical to letting the reader know, "I'm the neighborhood expert that you wouldn't want to buy or sell a home without, and here's how to contact me."

How do you make sure your blog is seen by others? Through social media, of course! Every blog post should be posted on all your social media accounts. Write a short description of the post and provide the link to the post itself, not the blog. Look into platforms and services like Hootsuite and IFTTT that will link your posts together, streamlining your online life.

A lot of people ask about personal vs. business pages on Facebook. My formula is to post my real estate-related postings on my Facebook business page, and keep my personal page, well, personal. If it's a really good real estate post, I share it from my business page to my personal page for a much softer plug to my friends. If you aren't keen on all of your clients seeing your personal page, direct them to your business page instead. For years I guarded my personal page, but now I see the value in letting all of my clients in. We have usually become friends anyway, so there is no harm, and this allows us to stay connected on a deeper level than a monthly newsletter or postcard provides. This will have to be a personal decision you make.

Blog posts and social media posts in general give a glimpse of your personality, and your personality is amplified through your pictures and the topics you post on your social media pages. Then along comes YouTube and other video sources to really kick it up a notch. It wasn't until April 2016 that you could stream a live video on your business Facebook page. Statistics show that people are ten times more likely to comment on a live video than on one that had been previously recorded and uploaded. This is huge news for agents wanting to engage their audience on Facebook! Can you imagine receiving ten times the number of client inquiries and leads due to simple live-streamed videos? This is where technology is taking us—be on board!

A video of you talking and showing what you're like outside of a carefully written post or posed picture gives your audience a whole new level of *you* to connect to. Use videos of you talking about the industry and local neighborhoods to draw in your audience and make them want to meet you in person.

Many sellers expect to see their homes on YouTube. All the videos that you can create—personal or listing-based—should be shared on your website and your social media accounts; they all tie together.

Every new listing I get, every new video and virtual tour I create, goes to my business page. I'm also sure to post those links on my lesser-used social media accounts, or I allow Hootsuite to do the work for me. If you aren't posting your listings you're going to have some disappointed clients on your hands— especially your social media-savvy ones. Show them that you're giving their home maximum exposure through the use of social media. Will a house sell from a Facebook post? Maybe not. But it does help boost interest in the property and get more people to click through your links to your IDX, where they then become leads. And if you show-and-tell by sending your seller links to the marketing you've done online for their property, your client will value the communication and can help spread the word about you to their SOI.

Linking your blog posts to your social media accounts increases traffic to the blog, thus helping it in the search engine ranks, which in turn will get even more eyes on your blog. Remember, you have to have a CTA so that you can turn your blog traffic into leads! Your CTA always needs to include ways to contact you. You can do the same with your videos, and embed them on your website. Running Facebook ads (linked to Instagram) on your blog posts and videos have high ROI, even with a tiny budget. Ads reach people outside of your page likes and SOI. This is why creating something of interest, showing your personality so people can connect to you, and having a CTA are so important. People have to feel compelled to click on your ads and have a way to contact you.

Whether you like it or not, it's human nature to have more confidence in an individual just because other people like him/her. So if your social media accounts look wimpy, beef up your likes and followers either through connecting with people you already know or running ads to boost your page. If a potential client is stalking you and your competitors online, it'll be in your favor to have a couple hundred likes on your business page, versus another agent who has only nine likes. This is called social proof and you need to make sure you've been vouched for!

You can consider other platforms and opportunities such as guest blogging, profile engagement on sites like Zillow where they allow you to answer customer questions, and local forums like City-Data. Many agents have built credibility for themselves and successfully find clients through these platforms. Also, there are multitudes of ways to advertise your business online through paid ads (Google Ads, for example). These are all tactics that can boost your online presence, but depend heavily on your time and budget. If you integrate any of these tactics into your Internet/social media component, be sure to include them on your schedule so they become methodical and not something that overwhelms your time. Also, keep a close eye on your budget (for anything you have to pay for) and analyze if you're receiving enough ROI.

Connect with Your Audience

Engage your audience with CTA in your posts (when appropriate) and follow up with comments and likes when they do respond. Posting content for your audience to connect with you is equally important as connecting to your audience in *their* lives and posts. Don't let your relationship be one-sided; comment on their posts, as well. Comments will always give you more credit than likes, by the way.

Many of my clients have come from my Facebook friends. Some were people I hadn't seen since high school 10-15 years ago. (If you're trying to guess my age, I got into this business eight years after high school and have been in it for more than twelve years . . . and just stop, it's not polite to ask a woman's age!) Some clients have been newer connections, and because of Facebook, we stayed in communication and I earned their business. If you were to take a peek at my personal Facebook page, you wouldn't see a whole lot about real estate. So how do I get these clients? By seeing what they post, what they have going on in their lives, and commenting. This doesn't mean you jump out of the bushes like a tiger on a rabbit when someone posts, "We're moving! Do you know of any agents?" No. You need to be more present and helpful in their lives or else you're going to come off as insincere. If you see a post about someone's new Etsy shop, then comment and share to support them. Learn how you can genuinely benefit the people you're connected to online and you'll be seen as sincere, and your efforts will pay off in the form of closings.

Give your audiences chances to connect with you and invite

them via social media to your events, such as open houses, home-buying seminars, and even a live stream video event.

Take connecting a step further and connect offline as well. When your friend posts on Facebook about her sick child, send over chicken noodle soup and a get well card. When a former colleague posts about a job promotion, send over a bottle of champagne. People blast information about their lives, sometimes too much, on social media so take those opportunities and not only show support online, but find ways to move your support to the real world.

Lastly, add everyone from your social media world into your database. Grow your database by sharing a link to your email newsletter on your website and social media accounts and allow people to opt-in to receive emails.

Managing Your Time

Through connecting your blog posts to your Facebook page, and your YouTube videos to your blogs (and another half dozen combinations of interweaving your online presence), you create a consistent, multi-platform online persona that allows buyers and sellers to get a feel for who you are and how you do business. When a buyer or seller searches for a neighborhood expert online and is led to your site or profile, they should be able to see all that you've posted online—this creates your online résumé. All your past listings will be showcased on your YouTube account, they can scroll through your many blog posts about the area, and they can view your social proof through page likes and followers.

Use these strategies and you will have created a strong online presence that gives you professional credibility and can earn you leads. Your online exposure is so critical for creating new leads and keeping you fresh in front of your database that it needs to be a daily part of your schedule.

But beware! If you spend too much time on, um . . . I'll *randomly* choose Facebook, your time will be swallowed and you'll be left feeling unbalanced *and* unproductive. The key is to set up a system so that you are present online and present in the other areas of your business. Here is a simple list of when and how often to post online:

- With each listing: Write a blog entry with photos, and then link it to social media. Create video on YouTube and add the link to your blog entry in the video description, then post to social media and embed in your website (either in a designated video page or in the blog). Make sure to post all material to social media (professional photos, virtual tour). As you have open houses, post them to social media and create an announcement (blog post) on your website.

- When working with buyers: Try to write a blog entry for each neighborhood you spend time in and then share it on social media. Go a step further and create a video of the neighborhood—and share it on your site and on social media. This will be a longer process, as you may show many neighborhoods on a single day, even. Set a goal such as one new neighborhood entry/video per week. After one year, you'll have 52 posts from this exercise alone!

- For each open house (when you're not the listing agent): Post all open houses on social media (follow the marketing plan given in *Your Key to Open House Success*). Write a blog post about the neighborhood and share it on social media.

- Monthly or quarterly: Do a video and/or blog entry about the current state of the market. Share those on social media.

- Every day: Set aside no more than 30 minutes to an hour for connecting with your SOI on social media. I prefer to do this with my morning coffee and before I begin my database calls. Make sure to genuinely comment on your friends' posts and see if there are ways you can help people each day. Discipline yourself with this time—don't allow half an hour to turn into half a day! Post interesting content, like running a 5K for a local charity, or finding a new favorite local restaurant, but stay away from controversial or annoying posts that can turn off your audience. (I know some of you are going to say, "If they don't like me for me, then I don't want them as a client anyway!" Well, if you are okay with limiting your income because it's important to you to rant on a hot topic issue, or your opinion on a presidential candidate's personal life, then by all means, limit your income. Remember, you are a business—you are selling YOU, your services, to your audience with every interaction, and whether you like it or not, people are judging if they would want to do *business* with you based on how you present yourself in your personal life.)

Find a flowchart of this list at:

http://www.ShannonEnsor.com/realestatemachine/ resources/

Just as a coach doesn't go into a game without a plan, you should not approach your career without a plan. If you know every step you take online helps you connect with people, increase your exposure or gain leads, you are following the right game plan.

Before I move on to the next chapter, and since this component is technology-related, I'd like to mention that the next big thing in real estate will undoubtedly be virtual reality (VR). Although I have yet to experience VR, some companies are already using VR with property tours for their high-end properties. Showing homes to buyers will reach a whole new level, one in which your clients from other states and countries will be able to tour homes without ever meeting you. You'll be expected to take your listing marketing to a higher level, too, with VR. But think also to the possibilities you'll have to grow your business and reach new clients through your personal marketing done via VR. It's going to be an exciting time, so be on the lookout now for ways to integrate VR into your business, and tout your use of it on your website and social media accounts.

Chapter 6
Farming

TOO MANY AGENTS WAIT TO DO geographic farming until their income hits a certain level, or when they procure a listing in a neighborhood. I'm going to show you why you need to integrate farming into your business, no matter what stage of the business you are in.

Here's an easy way to think of farming: a farm feeds you. Think of a farm in a traditional sense—the kind with livestock, vegetables and grains. Through consistent tending to his farm, a farmer produces the food his family needs (or income from selling his product). If he neglects his farm, even for a season, his family faces starvation and poverty. Sure, he can go down the road to his neighbor's house and ask for food, or use savings to buy food from the grocery, but he is no longer producing income for his family. A farm dies when it's left unattended and is no longer a source of food or income for the farmer.

Your real estate farm is *food* for your business. Over time, the people in your farm will churn—meaning, for most neighborhoods, there is a turnover of residents leaving and coming into the community. Neighborhoods naturally have a constant ebb and flow. Your goal is to be in the path of that ebb and flow so you can get *fed*.

Why do so many agents ignore this component of their career? Because farming costs money. When compared to an agent's sweet spot, their database, a farm is a financial commitment. Remember, an agent's database is the easiest, most nurtured area of their business. The people in your database will only buy and sell so often, and you cannot always rely on them for referrals. What must agents do to make sure they have a consistent book of business? The answer: farm.

I can hear some of you now: "Well, Shannon, I must disagree with you. My database is my sole source of business and they send me referrals all the time. In fact, it never fails, as soon as I think I'm about to hit a slow period someone in my database calls up to say they need to move! Besides, I don't need to spend a lot of money on my database because they already love me, and I hear farming is expensive."

Is that person you? Read the paragraph again slowly. Did you catch it this time? "...about to hit a slow period..." What if you never had to face a slow period or drought? This is why a farm is so important to your business: it gives you another avenue of business so you don't have to rely on your database alone.

How to Farm

Don't worry, I'm not going back to livestock and vegetables. But, through talking with many agents, I've learned that most agents don't know how to farm correctly. They bounce from farm to farm and lack consistency. They feel the pain of pouring money into a source that doesn't give any returns. Thankfully, there is a solution to this.

Key components of a farm:

- Location
- Consistency
- Multi-faceted

Location. A farm must be carefully chosen with the goal of sticking with it for many years. Do not pick a farm thinking, *I'll try this one for a while, then in a few months I'll change my farm to another community to see which I like better.* Your time and money will be wasted with this thinking.

Instead, pick a community you *desire* to farm, a community you know you can be passionate about. For some agents, the easiest community to be passionate about is the one they already live in. Or perhaps it is one they grew up in, and have nostalgia for. Or the one that, when their real estate career takes off, is their ideal 'move-up' community. If you are passionate about the community you farm, you increase your chance of keeping up with your farm for a longer period of time.

Of course, you must also look at your budget. How much will you set aside each month for your farming materials? Decide now and update as you reevaluate your goals and budget. Your budget determines the *size* of your farm.

Once you know the size of your farm—for example, you've determined your budget is enough to mail 200 postcards each month—it's time to pick your crop. A good rule of thumb is to search the tax records and pull only the homeowners who have lived in their homes at least three years and fewer than seven.

This is the sweet spot for people who tend to move more often. If you find that your target community has a different turnover rate, adjust accordingly. If you want a niche in your farm, such as only elderly people, you can further narrow your 'crop' to only single-story homes, since those tend to be more popular with the aging population. Play around with the parameters of your farm until you get a list of 200 (or however many you chose) who become your crop, or farm base.

Your farm base represents the people you most consistently target throughout the year, for budgeting purposes. If your budget allows you to do print marketing, such as magazines, local store ads, or even billboards, your farm is the place to do this. Of course, this means you will be reaching more than the 200 farm base you are specifically targeting, and that is a great thing. Now you will have exposure in front of those 200, plus their neighbors. Focus all your advertising in your farm, so you can double-up on your rate of return.

To illustrate what I mean by doubling-up, if you advertise in the high school football schedule for a school across town from your farm, you're missing out on the double exposure you could receive if you advertised with a high school in your farm, since at least 200 of those people are receiving your monthly postcards. By spending your advertising budget exclusively on your farm, you eliminate throwing money away on ads that don't work, and you set a disciplined structure that keeps you on track to success.

Consistency. In real estate, like most entrepreneurial businesses, the biggest barrier to success is fear. With farming, agents fear that they will be throwing their money away. This fear keeps them from putting the wheels in motion and dominating their farm. If you want to dominate a farm, all you need is commitment and consistency. Commit to your farm. Commit to mailing your specified number of cards each month to your farm, and never relent. Label your monthly mailer costs in your budget as a non-negotiable business expense. The month that you stop reaching your farm is the month you've thrown out all the money you've spent on it so far.

Yes, this means mailing *something* to your farm once a month. Hopefully, they are also seeing you in other advertising outlets throughout their community. In fact, this monthly postcard is just a small fraction of what they should receive from you, and I'll go over the other items in a moment. This monthly consistency gives you a compounding effect in your farm's minds, and that compounding effect is what gives you credibility as the neighborhood expert.

It is true: you can be the best agent in the world, but when pitted against the neighborhood expert that the sellers feel like they *know* because they have received a mailer from them once a month for the last four years, you're going to face stiff competition.

Do you ever wonder why an awful agent still gets so much business in a community? Take Awful Andy the Agent, for example. He's quite often seen driving with road rage around town, he dresses sloppily, and anytime you've been on a transaction with him, his attitude makes you wonder if he even likes being in this business. Yet his "For Sale" signs dominate a particular neighborhood, and that car he is driving is quite nice. You wonder, how is *he* so successful? He has consistently farmed that neighborhood, and through that consistency he has given those residents the impression that he is the go-to agent for the neighborhood. When a seller doesn't have a connection to another agent, who do they turn to? They turn to Awful Andy, whose postcard is on their mail table each month.

Even a newly-licensed agent can create the appearance of being a neighborhood expert through consistent targeting in a farm. If residents reliably see your marketing material claiming you are the neighborhood expert, they will begin to believe it, no matter how many sales you have under your belt. I see it happen all the time. A new agent with a planned budget and sheer determination to be a rising star in her farm starts methodically sending postcards to the same people, month after month. Soon, one "For Sale" sign pops up with her face on it . . . then another . . . and another. If you thought about farming that same neighborhood, but hesitated out of fear, you'll wonder, how did *she* do it? All it took was her commitment to consistency.

A note on postcards: I mention postcards as the source of your monthly farm mailer. This isn't simply an example of the kind of thing you might mail, it's your smart choice. Postcards allow you to plaster your logo and branding on two sides, so that no matter what, you can make an impression on the receiver. Even if your postcard takes a one-way trip from the mailbox to the garbage can with no layovers on the kitchen counter, you at least get a few seconds to put your name, logo and picture in front of the recipient. Whether they keep your material around or not, you are becoming a familiar face to them, and you are developing your name recognition. As for the material on your postcards, give your recipients relevant market information, along with a call to action. When a homeowner first gets the thought to sell his home, he'll start paying attention to the market information you're consistently sending, and you'll be the first name on his mind to call and set up the listing appointment.

Multi-Faceted. What if there are already five other agents farming the neighborhood you want to farm? Do you give up and decide to farm somewhere else, somewhere you don't feel as passionate about? No. First, they may not be as consistent as you. Second, word may get out that Awful Andy is, well, awful. And third, you're going to be multi-faceted in your approach to your farm in a way that cannot be exactly duplicated by other agents, giving you a competitive edge.

We've already discussed that any print or other media advertising should be focused in your farm. How else can you become multi-faceted in your farm? The secret: through using the other components of your business, including:

- Open houses
- Online/social media
- Database
- FSBOs/expireds
- Other (events, seminars, etc.)

Using these together will result in the other component of your business: working with buyers and sellers.

Open houses. We'll discuss open houses in depth in the next chapter, but I can't say it too often: to get the most out of your open houses, focus them in your farm. When you do this, the people in your farm and their neighbors will see your open house signs each weekend, receive your open house marketing materials, and even get to know you in person if they decide to drop by one of your open houses. Open houses give you a reason to contact your farm more often than your once-a-month postcards.

Online. Your next outreach comes from the Internet. On your website you should have blog posts about your farm. Take it a step further and post videos of you *in* the community, talking about the community. Create a fan page for your community on social media (as far as I know this mainly works with Facebook). Now your farm can search the community's name online and your posts and videos will pop up. And now you have another excuse to send something to your farm: an invitation to join the community page you created so that they can stay connected to their neighbors.

Database. If anyone in your SOI or database resides in your farm, move them to the very top of your database list. They are now your star! Build on the friendships and connections they have in the community through social events and networking. Show your star some love and make sure you never forget a birthday, special occasion, or just a random "it's been a while, let's have coffee" date. This star opens pathways to warm referrals *within* your farm, and therefore is a hot commodity to you. Other star database members in your farm are local business owners. Capitalize on the win-win relationship you can provide for local business owners who also thrive off of referrals within the community. You can suggest event sponsorships or freebies for newcomers to your area.

FSBOs/expireds. When working a farm, you should know it like the back of your hand. Blog posts, videos, open houses— all these things will keep you fresh and in tune with your neighborhood. Your knowledge of and work within your farm gives you the perfect reason to contact every FSBO and expired listing located in your farm and its surrounding areas. You have an easy in with these guarded sellers, since you are actively working their community and very well may bring a buyer. When they are ready to list (again), you will be in the forefront of their minds.

Other. Outside of monthly postcards, optional print advertising (football schedule ads, billboards, neighborhood newsletters/magazines, etc.) and the exposure you'll receive in your farm through the other areas of your business, you can connect to your farm in fun and creative ways. Hosting a class on loan programs, where you invite a lender to do most of the talking, is a direct way to get in front of your farm as an agent. But you can also farm in a not-so-direct way by creating or sponsoring events such as breakfast with Santa, movies in the park, creative market night where residents can showcase and sell their products, canned food drives, and a pumpkin patch. Combined with the monthly postcards that have valuable market information and your active involvement in your farm, you are enforcing what your farm sees on your postcards: you are the neighborhood go-to agent!

When you tackle your farm using the multi-faceted approach described above, you will earn an advantage over your competitors. Schedule these farming activities on a weekly basis, or as they apply, so you have a visual tool to confirm you're doing the necessary work to be successful in your farm. If you don't have a visual schedule and simply run your farm haphazardly, you'll get the same results as the farmer who randomly fertilizes and seeds his farm.

Plan your schedule each week, look at what has been working within your farm (based on leads and closings), and tackle any weaknesses you find. Update the budget for your farm periodically (every four months is ideal), so your business can continually grow along with you.

Chapter 7
Open Houses

SO FAR, THE MAIN COMPONENTS of a successful real estate career that I've mentioned—working with buyers and sellers, database, Internet/social media, and farming—are areas that most agents either already utilize to some degree or plan to when they have a larger budget. Open houses, although equally important as the others, attract controversy and I've noticed a distinct line drawn in the sand where agents are either pro- or anti-open house.

Why should open houses be considered an equal to database, farming, and the rest? Agents on the 'anti' side of the line argue that they can have a successful business without open houses. Some even argue that open houses are a waste of time for the seller and listing agent, and are mere tactics for buyer agents to gain business.

But those of us on the 'pro' side understand the answer to the question: open houses are critical to lead generation, database growth, and neighborhood credibility. They also contribute to the other components, allowing you to work smarter.

- Open houses help you generate leads and grow your database.

- Strategically holding open houses in your farm boosts your neighborhood visibility and credibility.
- Open houses give you a foot in the door with FSBOs and expireds.
- Blog posts and Facebook ads about your open houses help generate Internet leads and strengthen your credibility as an agent across your social media platforms.
- Open houses put you directly in front of the buyers and sellers you want to work with.

The open house component is not a tactic. It's not something to try out every now and then when your business is slow. Open houses boost your other components, giving you a strong, well-rounded business. If you leave out or haphazardly do open houses, you have a weakened, vulnerable business and you are not reaching your full potential in your career.

To achieve a well-rounded career you must view each component of your business as an intertwining mechanism that enhances the others, rather than taking away from the others. The dynamic power of the open house is your secret weapon to creating that thriving business you crave.

In my book, *Your Key to Open House Success*, I provide a detailed, day-by-day marketing plan for your open houses. The marketing plan I created doesn't simply show you how to prepare and plan for your open houses, it shows you how you can leverage each open house to create neighborhood credibility and increase your database growth. And guess what? The strategies you learn are integrated with the business-building aspects of farming, social media/online and FSBOs/expireds! This is how powerful the open house component of your business is.

Think of open houses as your prospecting super power. No other area of your business puts you face-to-face with buyer and seller leads. Working with buyers and sellers is an important component in which you are directly working with—you guessed it—buyers and sellers, but if you aren't prospecting for new leads, your closings will dwindle.

If you haven't utilized open houses up to this point (first, run and get my book so you can learn to do them the *right* way), you have probably experienced slow periods in your career. You cover enough floor duty shifts, or you've allocated a chunk of your budget toward advertising and farming, or maybe you pay a monthly service for Internet leads . . . but you still have that nagging feeling that you're missing the key to success in this business. Concern about the number of closings you'll have three months from now is the tell-tale sign that you lack balance in your career. Open houses can put you back on the track to success.

To illustrate the power of open houses, take a look at Amy Agent's real estate career so far. In Amy's first year in business, she had one closing, making approximately $4,000. Year two, she tripled her closings and income ($12,000). In her second year she got the courage to do open houses, but they were just from her office's roster. They were at two separate addresses, on different sides of town. While she had a couple of visitors at one of her open houses, the other produced none. She was unable to convert anyone from her first open house into a lead, and she kept forgetting to add those visitors into her database. She decided open houses just weren't for her. Luckily for Amy, her SOI warmed up to her becoming an agent and that's where her closings came from in that second year.

Frustrated and under pressure from her husband to either make more money in real estate or switch back to nursing, Amy decides to change brokerages in year three. Her new manager teaches her the principles from *Your Key to Open House Success* and Amy now has a whole new outlook on open houses.

She chooses a listing in her target neighborhood, one in which she hopes to farm when her budget is larger, because this is her dream neighborhood with the school system she wishes her children to attend one day. She markets through writing a blog post about the open house on her new website, posting the blog entry and open house details on her Facebook page and asking her local friends to please 'share' the post, and walking door-to-door in her target neighborhood with 200 invitations to her open house. In one month, Amy holds that same open house three more times. One month and four open houses later, she has two listings from her marketing efforts within her targeted neighborhood, three new buyer-contracts from leads she picked up at her open houses, nine more potential buyers that she's sending listings to, and a Facebook friend from out-of-state has sent her a referral because she was impressed with Amy's online campaigns. She is diligent about adding her open house leads into her database, which has grown significantly over the span of one month. Amy is confident in where her next three months of closings are coming from and will continue leveraging open houses in her target neighborhood into more buyer and seller leads to sustain her momentum. Her income this year is on track to clear more than $60,000—a huge jump from her meager beginnings as an agent. Through open houses alone, this year she'll add more than 160 people to her current database of 50 people—that's more than triple! Her credibility as the neighborhood expert will also increase through the listings she's received from open house leads and through her consistent open house presence. The power of open houses turned her career around, and it can do the same for you.

Can you relate to Amy's story? I can. In fact, her first two years of real estate were an awful lot like my first year, except I flailed and failed at more than two open houses that year. Her third year looks a lot like my career once I put a system in place for my open houses (and each year my income builds upon itself as Amy's did, never dropping below six figures due to the systems I have in place).

If you've started out like Amy and I did, trying an open house here and there, and the only result you had was frustration, make sure you are applying the correct strategies to each open house. More importantly, make sure that you stick with them. Just like with Internet leads and your farm, this is a numbers game, and you have to be in it to win it! The more open houses you do, the larger your database will grow and the stronger your neighborhood credibility will become.

One Event, Five Days of Planning

If you wait until the last minute to commit to an open house, you'll likely fill that spot in your schedule with something else. Plan six days in advance for your open houses and persistently commit to this prospecting activity. Your strategic planning starts on Tuesday of each week, and is spread out throughout the week so you don't become overwhelmed while staying on top of your marketing. A Tuesday start also ensures you have maximum time to attract leads.

As mentioned in the previous section, focus your open houses in communities that are either your farm, next to your farm, or are considered move-up/move-down to your farm. Instead of spreading yourself thin over your entire city, home in on where you really want business so that your concentrated efforts lend you expert credibility in your target neighborhoods.

What do you do if you have a listing in a different area than one you'd like to target or farm? Ask another agent in your office to hold the listing open while you hold open a listing in or near your farm. This allows your listing to receive the important marketing exposure it needs, and you can focus on drumming up more business in your target neighborhoods.

Once you have your address for your open house targeted, you then tour the home, doing reconnaissance work for your blog post and Facebook posts and ads. While in the neighborhood, put together your plan for your open house directional signs and locate any FSBOs. Before Tuesday ends, you should have a blog post written on the open house and/or neighborhood and a Facebook ad set to invite people based on their location, and perhaps interests (such as "golf course" or "lake"—yes, somehow Facebook has data-mined details like this, making it possible to be specific with your ads . . . both wonderful and scary!).

I take Wednesdays off from my open house planning, but I'm back at it Thursdays and Fridays, going door-to-door with invitations and speaking with FSBOs and expireds. This work can sometimes be condensed into one day, depending on your speed and the number of homes you target, and the number of FSBOs/expireds available to speak with.

Saturday morning is reserved for getting open house material ready to go, which includes updating a neighborhood market analysis, and then Sunday is open house day. You are marketing yourself just as much as the listing at each open house, so be sure to put your best foot forward when it comes to your appearance, the appearance of the material, and the treats you pass out to guests.

By breaking down the tasks into this day-by-day schedule, you can successfully plan for your open house and still have time for your other components, such as showing homes to buyers. More importantly, when you realize that your planning does double-duty with your other components, you become more purposeful with your time and have greater focus on growing your business.

Chapter 8
FSBOs/Expireds

IF I TOLD YOU I KNOW OF A STEADY STREAM of sellers that come from an ever-replenishing source, would you say, "Sign me up!" or would you run away in a zig-zag pattern ensuring I wouldn't be able to catch you if I tried? I bet it's the former, and you've already pulled out pen and paper to take notes.

Now, when I tell you that this never-ending lead source is from FSBOs and expireds, how do you feel?

Ready to run again? Do images of vultures—agents who wait for other agents to fail so they can swoop in and grab the scraps—pop into your head? You probably imagine these vultures hovered over an austere desk, a phone in one hand for cold calls and stamps in another so they can get their sales letters out before all the other agents working the same leads. These agents work FSBOs and expireds out of *desperation*. They throw a lot of darts at the board and hope to hit the target every now and then. As I've mentioned before, real estate is a numbers game and you have to be in it to win it, so at least they have that principle covered. What you want to avoid is making FSBOs/expireds your only prospecting focus, and you must take out the cold factor and replace it with a warmer approach.

You probably also imagine hostile sellers on the receiving end of any FSBO or expired communication. That image is enough to make any thin-skinned agent run away screaming! So why am I being so mean and insisting that you must work among the vultures and cross enemy lines in order to have a balanced, successful real estate career? I promise, I'm not a mean person! I do this because I know there are different ways, *better* ways, to handle FSBOs and expireds.

When handled properly, FSBOs and expired listing leads become a strong staple in your real estate machine that you *enjoy* prospecting for and working with. There is a never-ending supply of FSBOs and expired listings, and if you consistently work those leads you'll have a never-ending supply of listing sources.

In the last chapter I briefly discussed how open houses feed into the FSBO/expired component of your business. I'd like to dive in a little deeper so you can learn how to effectively use open houses to turn those hostile sellers into your biggest fans. First, when you are scouting the neighborhood for your upcoming open house, you need to identify any FSBOs and expired listings nearby. Being the experienced agent that you are, you know that buyers at your open house will want to talk about the other available properties in the neighborhood, and are usually extra-intrigued by the FSBOs (due to lack of exposure online, buyers can't usually preview 25+ photos of FSBOs like they can with MLS-listed homes) and by any homes that recently dropped off the MLS without a "SOLD" sign ever appearing in the yard. These questions signal that you have an extremely serious buyer in front of you who has been stalking the neighborhood for their perfect home, or perhaps someone who may need some coaxing to jump off the fence to go through with a purchase. Being the prepared agent that you are (hint, hint), knock on the doors of those FSBOs and expireds to get their stories, tell them about your upcoming open house, and ask if you can get a tour of their homes in case interested buyers from your open house request information.

Instead of cold-calling these guarded sellers, you have given them a real reason you want to see their homes, and you have shown them you have *value* to bring—you aren't just giving them another sales pitch.

Then invite them to your open house so that they can see your high level of professionalism in action. Send them thank you notes for the tour, and direct them to your blog and Facebook posts about their neighborhood. Encourage them to share the posts about their neighborhood with their friends. Since you're targeting their neighborhood or the surrounding area, they should receive a new open house invite from you each week. You'll be on their radars and they will notice how active an agent you are—and how active you are in their neighborhood. You become the neighborhood expert in their eyes, and when they are ready to list or re-list, *you* are the agent they call—not one of the twenty agents who hounded them with cold calls but neglected to build a relationship with them or prove their credibility as the neighborhood expert. By the time they call you for the listing appointment, they are your biggest fans.

FSBOs and expireds don't have to be a scary component of your business, but instead should be seen as a natural part of your agent duties. You can incorporate FSBOs and expireds into your farming campaign and personally invite them to any neighborhood events or seminars you host. Invite them to share (or better yet, get their permission so you can share) their home's details on the neighborhood Facebook page you have created. Warmly approaching these lead sources is not only more enjoyable for you, but more successful than the cold calling approach.

Now that you're no longer running from these leads, let me show you why FSBOs and expireds are equal to the other five components I've discussed in this book.

Listing Leads Ripe for the Picking

In order to have more buyers and sellers to work with, you must always be prospecting, and the six components of your business work together to keep your machine running. Why do I list FSBOs/expireds as one of the six main components? First let's consider the elements discussed so far:

- Nurturing your SOI via your **database** acts as a funnel for your leads.
- Reaching your database **online**, and gathering new leads through your blog and Facebook posts and videos, keeps you visible. Your IDX solution on your website also generates buyer leads.
- **Farming** puts you consistently in front of homeowners who you *hope* will sell soon.

- **Open houses** give you buyer and seller exposure, but
  if you're not at the open house, another agent will be
  and the leads will go to them, not you.

In your business formula, FSBOs and expireds fill the hole where you need a constant flow of listing leads.

FSBOs and expireds are listings that are ripe for the picking. You know these people want to sell, and you know how to reach them directly. Approach them in the warm, value-adding manner I described in the previous section instead of as a vulture, and they become a rich lead source for you.

An agent confided in me over lunch one day that she was growing weary of the business because she seemed to only land buyer clients. Somewhere she had heard, "List to exist!"—words that stuck in her head and made her feel like a failure with each month that passed without a listing under her name. As much as I'd like to denounce that phrase because I witnessed how it haunted my friend and negatively affected her performance, there is some merit to it. You need listings in this business in order to have a well-balanced career (frazzled buyers agents will attest to that statement!).

Some agents think a "For Sale" sign in the yard is all they need to gain momentum in a neighborhood, as if the sign will magically multiply overnight. That is wishful thinking. It is the *work you produce* surrounding a listing that allows you to gain traction as a neighborhood expert and then gain more seller leads. Before you have a listing to showcase the hard work you're willing to put in, you must put yourself in front of ripe listing leads.

What better way to fill your listing roster than with those sitting ducks waiting for the right agent to sell them on the process and sell their home? If you're an unknown agent in a community, standing on the corner with a sign announcing, "Sell Your Home with Me!" won't gain you any listing leads . . . but warmly going to FSBOs and expireds will. Change your approach to these leads from cold to warm, and you'll see how a steady stream of FSBOs and expireds can supplement your income so that you aren't solely dependent on your database or farm for closings.

A side note about <u>withdrawn</u> listings: at my board, and most likely yours as well, we have another listing status called withdrawn. Many agents I know go after withdrawn listings as if they are expired listings. I caution you against this. While those agents argue that the listing agent may have quickly withdrawn the listing at the last moment of their listing agreement instead of allowing it to go "expired"—which does happen, despite the COE—there is a greater chance that the listing agent still has the listing and he and the seller have agreed to withdraw it from the MLS for a specific reason. For instance, at my board, if you move the listing to temporarily off market (T), the listing days on market (DOM) only go on a pause, and the count picks right back up when it goes active again. The home must be withdrawn for 90 days for the clock to go back to 0 DOM. If a seller wants his home off the market for the entire winter season and sees value in letting the counter reset to 0 DOM, yet still wants you to market the home off-MLS, you would choose the withdrawn (W) route of 'T'. Instead of violating the REALTOR® Code of Ethics (COE) and soliciting a seller who is potentially listed with another agent, contact the agent first to find out the story behind the 'W.' Be direct and ask them, "Do you still have the listing? Do the sellers still want to sell?" Most agents will not lie if they lost the listing and will tell you, "Good luck with that!" You may even find out more information, such as, "They decided to let the listing go because they called off the divorce and want to stay." Now you know to direct your efforts to the next expired listing on your list and you haven't violated the COE.

Chapter 9
Advertising and Tactics

I'VE SHOWN YOU THE SIX COMPONENTS of an agent's business that are critical to a well-rounded, successful career: working with buyers and sellers, database, Internet/social media, farming, open houses and FSBOs/expireds. But I know what you're thinking. "Hey! You left out _____. And I closed my last sale because of this other thing, _____." It is true; these six are not the be-all, end-all when it comes to the *source* of your closings. But they are the components every real estate professional should employ in order to have a well-rounded, successful business.

Four components help you bring in new leads, which funnel into your database and then turn into buyer and seller clients. Through consistency and a well-planned work week, you'll learn how to effectively balance those six areas of your business to become a top-producing agent in your market. Other items, which I am about to discuss, are either prospecting *tactics* or things that should be second-nature to you as a salesperson. While they can result in closings, they are supplemental to the main six components that agents need to focus on in their careers.

Self-Advertising

Many agents I speak to see self-advertising as the stand-alone, primary component of their business. They get so wrapped up in where and what they need to be advertising that it becomes their largest source of stress.

And how easy is it for us to become entangled in this advertising trap? Every day I receive several phone calls, too many emails to count (in the hundreds if you count my spam box), and my mailbox is stuffed with "opportunities" to advertise myself as an agent. Many of these calls are scams. In my early days as an agent, I spent hundreds of dollars on advertising in a high school football schedule, only to learn that the company was a scam and my face never appeared on the school's actual handouts. Others try to woo us by saying we can be one of the only agents in a particular zip code, *but you'd better act fast!*

Many of these attempts are easy to say no to, but the constant barrage leaves agents wondering if they really are doing all they need to advertise. They think, "Maybe if I just had my face in the latest luxury magazine, I'd get more leads this month." And while there is something to be said for some advertising, such as in the luxury home magazines, these avenues only pay off when you commit long-term. Unless you are a fixture in that magazine or on that billboard, you're wasting your money. Too many agents try an advertising avenue for a month or so and then stop. When they stop, the money they spent in the months prior is flushed down the drain. It's worth repeating: when it comes to self-advertising, you need long-term commitment so that you become a fixture, or else you are wasting your money.

If these questions burden your mind—*What other things should I spend my budget on? What else can I be doing to improve my success in this business?*—you'll lose focus on how to efficiently run your business, become frustrated, and possibly burn out of the business. Instead, stop viewing self-advertising as a component all on its own, but instead as something you do in conjunction with your other components of business. So how *should* you self-advertise?

- **Working with buyers and sellers**: You need to have a branding package in place. I'm not talking about folders with your company's logo on it (unless you are the broker/president of your company and you *are* the brand). As discussed in depth in Chapter 2, every agent needs a personalized branding campaign that allows their target market to connect with *them*, not their company. Your personality should radiate throughout your branding. Do you like building homes with Habitat for Humanity? Make sure your personality is a visible part of your branding, and feature a picture of you involved. All your marketing materials—pocket folders, letterhead, brochures—should feature your brand. With your branding package in place, you now have material ready to go when a new buyer wants to see a home, or a seller calls you for a listing appointment. The branded material will set you apart from your competition and increase your professionalism. Also, it helps you stay in your clients' minds longer; a company logo will only make your *company* stay in their minds. Make the impact count toward *you*. Your initial investment in the marketing company to create your brand, the professional photos of yourself, and the printing of the materials will be the largest part of your advertising budget spent in this category. But once it is created, it can and should be something you use for many years to come.

- **Database**: This is your advertising budget sweet spot! There is no better place to spend money than on the people who already know and like you, and are therefore more likely to use you every time they buy or sell a home! Outside of sending monthly postcards and email newsletters, advertising to your database can be the most fun part of your job. Did you know that taking your clients out for coffee is considered advertising? Just spending time with the people in your database is considered advertising yourself, even if you are like me and never let business talk go beyond casual. Create an annual client appreciation party that your database will look forward to attending year after year. Investing in your database will always be advertising dollars well spent.

- **Internet/social media**: If your budget allows, you can have an advertising campaign for your website. Your first question is whether you have a website robust enough to justify spending money to advertise. If your site lacks an IDX solution that allows leads to sign in and search for homes, the answer is no. Also, if you do not have a call to action on your site once you have attracted leads to it, then advertising your site will be a waste of money. If you have these necessary elements in place, how do you decide when to advertise? When do you stop feeling like there could be something more to do? This will depend on many factors that are unique to your market area. If you spend money on Google AdWords/Pay-Per-Click, will it make a noticeable difference and actually provide leads, or is your market already saturated with agents paying for space on page one? Adjust your budget for online advertising considering what works for you, move on, and evaluate quarterly. Obsessing over whether you are doing enough will only keep you in a rut. Notice I didn't say, "And make sure to sign up with every ad company that calls you promising to get you on the first page of Google"? That's right, because I didn't and you shouldn't!

More and more these days, and I'm sure this will continue to evolve as the online world does, it is becoming more cost-effective for agents to spend their marketing budget on social media rather than Google AdWords. Facebook ads are now integrated with Instagram, and you can use their analytics to target your audience. Your ads can run from general (such as, "Use our site to search for homes") to specific (such as ads for listings and open houses). Your goal is to determine your budget, reevaluate that budget quarterly, and feel good that you are working thoughtfully and professionally.

- **Farming**: Self-advertising in your farm includes 1) sending monthly letters or postcards, 2) announcing open houses, listings and buyer needs, 3) other seasonal bonus items, and 4) advertising in locations/publications targeted to your farm. All of these must display your branding, and you must be consistent with your messages. If you stop sending a monthly postcard after eight months, the money you spent for those eight months goes right down the drain. When you decide to farm a neighborhood, it is a marketing commitment that should not be taken lightly. Commit to a budget and a plan that includes the four areas mentioned above—the seasonal bonus items should not be optional! Think long-term with your farm and plan accordingly. Know from the outset if you plan to give away flags on the Fourth of July and mini-pumpkins in October. When you have a plan in place, you'll prevent the feeling of *am I doing enough? What else should I be doing?* When you work the **FSBOs/expireds** in your farm, the same self-advertising benefits apply.

- **Open houses**: You should host 40 open houses per year. Sound like a lot? Look at it this way: you'll have 12 weekends a year where you don't have to do an open house! That gives you a three-month break from open houses, although I suggest breaking up those three months throughout the year. (Pick up a copy of *Your Key to Open House Success* to learn the strategy behind the 40 open houses.) This means you have 40 open houses to budget: online ads, invitations and treats (yes, even treats are a form of marketing yourself; in this business, everything you do represents your level of professionalism).

Spend your money advertising in these areas and you will increase your leads, database, and number of closings month after month.

Marketing Your Listings

Listing marketing is another area that causes agents to feel overwhelmed. Even if a listing sells quickly, the agent may wonder, *Did I do enough with that listing to boost my business when I had the chance?* While this is not the time to go into detail about marketing your listings, I want to make sure you understand how you can leverage each listing to get more listings, with three simple rules.

Rule #1: *You don't have to reinvent the wheel when it comes to marketing your listings, just stay on top of new things coming out.* Take a look at what other successful agents are doing to market their listings, and emulate them. See a new trend coming out? Determine whether it can benefit your sellers or yourself and add it to your marketing plan. For example, drone photography/videography has become so popular these days, we now do it with all our listings. It costs a lot more, but it has become something that either our clients *expect* us to do, or that sets us apart from the competition. Also, drone footage brings in more leads because buyers and sellers see value in working with top-notch professionals who go above and beyond for their clients.

A team member recently came to me with a 3D flyer for his listing. I'm still on the fence about whether this is the "next big thing." It's high on the cool factor, but I'm unsure of the practicality of it and if recipients will even understand how to use it. If you see something new that listing agents are spending their marketing money on, don't be afraid to sit back and watch others use it for a short while first. Waiting helps you determine whether it is worth adding to your plan or if it is a money-wasting fad. And keep your eye out for ways to incorporate virtual reality! That is certainly the next big thing in real estate.

Rule #2: *Have a marketing plan in place that you will follow-through with regardless of 1) how long the listing takes to sell and 2) the list price.* Your listings are a portfolio of your work, and are used to get more business, whether intentionally or not. Make sure your portfolio is consistent and that each listing receives the royal treatment. Knowing that you committed 100% to each listing takes away the haunting question of whether you're capitalizing on every opportunity in this business. For example, if you've done all the marketing possible for a listing that sits with no offers, you know the problem doesn't exist with the home receiving exposure; the problem is with the price or condition of the home. This helps you sleep better at night and shows you where to tackle the no-offer problem with your clients. Also, if you follow through with your marketing campaign even though your listing goes under contract before you can even get it in the MLS, you not only live up to the commitment you've made to your seller, and will now receive a lifetime of referrals from them, but you have made sure to leverage that listing into listings when other people see your work in action. This also helps keep the buyers on their best behavior during any contingencies because they too will see you actively marketing the home they have put under contract, and they know others will be just as excited about the home as they were. No listing should be kept a secret! Commitment and follow-through will take you far in this business.

I have clients who shout how much they love me from the mountaintops because I gave them $1,000,000 service on their $100,000 home. Because I treat each home like a piece of my portfolio, every home receives the same marketing plan, complete with a staging appointment and professional photos/video. Yes, that means I do the exact same steps for a rural manufactured home as I do for a luxury home in West Austin. The result: a solid marketing plan that sells more homes, reaps me more referrals, and gives me confidence in my system. I never have the nagging feeling of *What else should I be doing to sell this home?*

Rule #3: *Boast to boost*. If I've done the above, then I'll receive referrals from happy clients and leads attracted by my marketing. That leaves one more wide open lane to bring in business: self-advertising. Make sure to tell your database, your social media followers, the people in your farm—everyone—anytime you sell a home. Each sale is a badge of honor, a mark of credibility that shows you are a great real estate professional. Use this to your advantage and don't keep your successes a secret.

Property Tours

Property tours are certainly not a primary component of your business, and can be over- or under-used by agents. Some agents can get caught in a cycle of attending property tour after property tour without ever participating in a real estate transaction. You have to make time to prospect for new clients and that's hard to do if you are always on a tour bus with a bunch of other agents. But you can and should use property tours to attract new clients.

When you go on a property tour, take pictures of any notable homes or features and take notes on the communities you visit. Upload the pictures to your social media accounts and show your sphere of influence that you are out in the field. Hashtag fan? Have fun with it: #propertytour #realtorlife #iknowmoreabouteastaustinthanyoudo. Then write a blog post about the communities you visited, making sure to share it to your social media accounts.

Use property tours to show people that you are an active agent, and what parts of town you are sharpening your knowledge in. Your posts will attract new leads and you'll stay fresh in front of your SOI.

Networking

Depending on your methods, networking can be a powerful way to receive leads and grow your database. The president of my company used to joke that I received all my business through happy hours. He wasn't far from the truth! My social butterfly personality made it easy to gain new friends through happy hours; I would naturally talk about my career and eventually my new friends called on me for their real estate needs.

However, there is a slight distinction between the way I network through happy hours and other networking methods. The people from my happy hours would fall under my database/

SOI, but happy hours are merely a means for me to stay in front of that database rather than a pointed networking effort. Sure, I grew my database through networking at happy hours (friends-of-friends becoming friends), but ultimately, for me the lines between happy hours, networking, and database become fuzzy (pun intended).

BNIs (Business Networking International) are a popular networking resource. Local BNI chapters meet monthly or weekly to allow members to showcase their services. Only one person per industry is allowed in the group—a huge benefit of the BNI—and members are strongly urged to refer business to each other. I've heard the good, the bad, and the ugly about BNIs and suggest that if you do find one you like, create one-to-one relationships with each of the members and truly become referral partners. This kind of networking is not included in my six major areas because you are relying on referrals from other people who are obligated under the BNI to send you business, but in reality they could have a close friend or family member they send their business to.

Some agents spend their time networking with other real estate professionals through a variety of agent-centric happy hours, builder-sponsored wine tours, etc. I've even had agents on my team turn down hot leads who were ready to see a home because they had to go to an agent happy hour! I cringe every time I think about it, but to be fair, there is a *small* reason these agents might attend these networking events. (PS, if you are attending these events without the following motivations, you are wasting your time—take the leads instead!) Agent-to-agent networking can be a healthy resource for referrals, especially when both agents strictly work a niche market and refer out all leads that don't fall under that niche. Also, if you become BFFs with a title sales representative who has a huge database in your town and needs an agent to send that business to, you are making a wise networking move. It's also possible that you build rapport with other agents at the events, giving you a leg up in multiple offer situations. Even if those things are true, don't rely heavily on this type of networking, as it will be the seller's ultimate decision to accept an offer, not the round of shots you bought his agent at last month's event. And if you aren't searching for referral connections at these events, go to a non-agent happy hour somewhere and grow *your* database!

Being Present in Your Life

Being present in your life is a little like networking. As a salesperson, you are your own product and everywhere you go, you need to be selling you. I'm going to use myself as an example. For the past four years I've lived in a community of about 4,200 homes. I moved in knowing no one on a social level. Now, I can't even pump gas without running into at least three people I know. Here's why:

- Fitness groups: my community is fitness-minded, and at any given point during the day there is a boot camp going on somewhere in my community. One of the first things I did when I moved into my community was to join a fitness group, which evolved into another group, then another group, then another group. Throughout my hour-long workouts I've gained dozens of friends. We all become Facebook friends, go to events together, etc.—fitness is social. I don't jump down their throats and talk about being an agent, but those things come up casually in discussions and whenever someone needs to sell or has a referral, I get a message.

- Mommy groups: I'm a mom, and the mommy group in my community is HUGE. Our community has three preschools, three elementary schools, one middle school, and the high school is not too far away. As you can imagine, we have a huge group and the influence of the mommies in my neighborhood is king . . . or I should say, queen. We're all connected on Facebook and through conversations during pick-up or drop-off in the halls of the schools. When I go to the grocery store, I inevitably run into at least three other moms and their children, and can ask if the baby has started teething yet; we are a caring group of women who look out for each other. This group also gathers at sporting events for our littles and school-related events. We become deeply involved in each other's lives. And, of course, they know what I do for a living.
- Church: I don't go to church advertising that I'm in real estate. However, the people I interact with at church get to know who I am, and my profession comes up naturally in conversation. Even if you don't attend a church, think about other areas of your life that you are involved in that include interacting with people.

Now these aren't my only three areas of "being present in my life," but they relate to how I immersed myself into my community and, as a result, have gained business. I must add that I did not do any of those three things just to get leads (goodness gracious, I certainly didn't have children just to get more leads!). No, they are all things I would've been passionate about being involved in, regardless of my profession. But since I show up to become connected to those around me, they get to know me and what I do for a living as a result. This is the natural ebb and flow of networking—or just being present in my life.

If you aren't a Christian mom who's into fitness and lives in a large neighborhood, there are options for you, too. Before we had children, my husband and I attended and hosted weekly poker parties. What are your hobbies or things outside of real estate that you are passionate about? Identify your passions and find a way to get social with them.

Do you go onto Facebook to rant about the President, or do you scroll through your friends' feeds to see what's going on in their lives? One will cause you to lose clients, the other will show you opportunities to receive clients. Being present in your life will show you ways you can help others, whether it is through bringing soup to a sick friend, or referring an agent to someone moving to and from states you don't work in.

Phone Duty/Floor Duty

Whether you refer to it as phone duty or floor duty, this is another tactic agents value as a main component in their career. In case you aren't familiar with floor duty, it is the sometimes mandatory time you spend at your office handling the phone leads that come into the main office line. Some offices also give in walk-in leads to the person covering floor duty, and some have a web lead system in place that routes to the agent on duty.

And boy, is floor duty coveted at my office! Shifts are taken as quickly as the schedule is posted. Agents have their preferred or 'lucky' time slots, and there is a great deal of strategy used with floor duty. And, no doubt, floor duty is a good tactic to receive leads.

So why do I not include floor duty as a main component of your business? Because with floor duty you are simply fielding leads that your brokerage has worked hard to funnel into the main office line. You are not building *your* business with floor duty, but merely supplementing your leads. Building *your* business requires getting **your** name into the community, becoming known as the go-to agent within **your** SOI and your farm, making **your** presence known online. Building **your** real estate business. Fielding leads from your broker is a great tactic to help build your database and get in front of buyers and sellers, but your main focus needs to be on building your business.

I do have a solid piece of advice for your floor duty: when a caller asks you a question about a property, don't simply answer and let your lead hang up because they no longer need anything from you. Engage them in a conversation geared at meeting in person. For example, when they ask how many bedrooms a home has, don't stop at, "Four." Instead say, "Four. How many bedrooms do you/does your family need?" And when they ask for the price of a home, you answer, "Five hundred thousand. Is that in your preferred price range?" Next you follow their responses with either, "Great, are you available this evening or tomorrow afternoon to view the home?" Or, "I understand this home isn't in your preferred price range, how about I send you a list of homes in the $X range and we can get together sometime this week to view them. What is your email address?"

There are many great books written on scripts, such as Tom Hopkins' *The Art of Selling Real Estate*. Study scripts and become comfortable with the language of them so you can sound polished and natural with a phone lead.

Seminars

There is a plethora of seminars you can hold as an agent. A few ideas are:

- First-time Home-buying Tips (works great in apartment complexes)
- Fight Your Property Taxes
- Decluttering 101 *or* Hottest New Home Trends
- Home Maintenance 101
- Feng Shui for Your Home

You don't have to be good at public speaking to host seminars. Instead, bring in professionals you have developed relationships with, such as lenders, home stagers, and inspectors, to do the presentation for you. As long as you introduce yourself and the speaker, have marketing material for the attendees, brand yourself in the advertising for the event and stick around after to mingle with attendees, you're on the right track and can avoid lengthy speeches that may give you the hives.

The two benefits of these seminars are to gain name recognition in a community (so they are most effective when held in a community you are farming) and to create relationships with the attendees that allow you to add them to your database. Unless you go wild and schedule a seminar every week of the year (with 52 seminars, if you connect with at least four people on average at each one, you will grow your database by more than 200 people in a year—wild!), you should not consider this a main component of your business. Due to unpredictable turnout and the high costs associated with room rentals and refreshments, most agents will not perform many of these a year, making seminars more of a tactic than a main component. You will receive more return on investment with the six major components of your business.

Housewarming or Bon Voyage Parties

Housewarming or bon voyage parties are a wonderful database tactic that should certainly be utilized, though not considered a component of your business. After a buyer purchases a home, ask to throw them a housewarming party. You provide the food and do the legwork of sending out invitations, making it easier on the homeowner after their hard work of moving into the home. With sellers, you do the same except before they move out, invite their neighbors, friends and family over to help them say goodbye to their home—and again, you provide food and are in charge of sending invites.

Through the invitation process, you have taken one person in your database and added their entire database to your own. Talk about leverage! You send invites with your branded stationary, listing you, the agent, as the host/hostess. Of course, assuming you did a great job for your clients, they will spend the party bragging about your wonderful service to the people who like and trust them—this is the power of third-person credibility. You won't have to talk about how great you are, your clients will do it for you! You **must** follow through and add these people to your database so they hear from you on more than one occasion after the party (your thank-you note). Again, this is a fun and credibility-adding tactic that will increase your database, but is not a main component of your business.

Education

Does this topic come as a surprise to you? We all have periodic education requirements to fulfill in order to keep our licenses active. How do you tackle your classes—online or in a classroom? I firmly believe in showing up to classes for my education requirements because I get to hear the instructor's stories and anecdotes. When I was a new agent, I learned more from the teachers at my continuing education classes—and their horror stories of what *not* to do as an agent—than I learned from the first company I worked with. I know some of you just want to get the requirement over with as fast as possible with those online courses, where you can simply hit enter four hundred times while barely looking at the screen, but you will get so much more out of physically attending classes.

How does education get you leads (besides allowing you the right to keep your license active)? Through social media. This is why you shouldn't see education as a full component of your business, but you can convert this necessary task into a tactic. While at your classes, tweet, post on Facebook, or use whatever social media you like best, about what you are learning. Show your followers that you place your education as a priority to help serve their needs best! Then, take something you learned from class, or a teacher's anecdote, and blog about it. For example, if you haven't yet had to experience what happens when a seller tries to back out of selling, and you hear an intriguing and educational story from your MCE teacher, go home and blog about what you learned about how sellers should act in this situation. This positions you as an industry expert and lends you credibility in front of your blog readers and database (because you should send out a link to your blog post to your database, as well as share it on social media, including Facebook, Twitter, and LinkedIn).

There comes a point when you can *over-educate* yourself, meaning you spend so much time in classes that you never go into action. Your best education will come from experience, so don't be afraid to jump in with both feet. Physically go to your required classes, earn credentials such as GRI (Graduate Realtor Institute), ABR (Accredited Buyers' Representative) and CNE (Certified Negotiation Expert), share your knowledge with others, and place your priority on prospecting for clients!

Chapter 10
Implementation

NOW THAT YOU UNDERSTAND that a well-rounded, successful real estate career is based on the six components—working with buyers/sellers, building and nurturing your database, Internet/ social media, farming, open houses and FSBOs/expireds—and that there are supplemental tactics you can employ, it's time to discuss proper implementation.

Proper implementation comes from organizing and managing your schedule, monitoring what you're doing right and adjusting when you need improvement, and learning to use the components together so you can work smarter.

If you're wondering if the six components apply to you, or if they could even transform your career, ask yourself if any of these statements ring true:

- You skip from one focus to another, often dropping the past focus altogether. For example, you start up a farm, invest in sending mailers for six months, and then hear about a new web lead program and drop your farm so you can invest in the program.

- You don't know where your closings will come from three months from now.

- You've decided _____ just doesn't work for *you*. Perhaps it's open houses. You've tried a few and decided they weren't worth your time and have cut them out altogether.

- There aren't enough hours in the day or days in the week or money in your bank account.

- You contemplate a second job or getting out of the business.

- You jump from brokerage to brokerage, trying to fix *your* lack of business.

Are you ready to become a successful real estate agent? It's time to drop the excuses and properly implement the necessary components that will create the success you crave.

Organizing and Managing Your Schedule

The first thing you need to do is to time-block your daily schedule. I recommend Michael Maher's *Seven Levels of Communication* because it provides excellent detail on how to efficiently time-block your schedule. When I sit down with agents to discuss their schedules, we look at the following and decide where/when in the week these fit in their schedules:

- Time spent driving buyers around to homes and writing contracts

- Listing appointments and the preparation for a listing appointment; time spent marketing listings
- Open house—preparation and hosting
- Contacting their database
- Tending to their farm
- Online time, both for writing a blog post and hanging out on social media
- Time spent building rapport with FSBOs and sellers of expired listings
- Other real estate-related items (time to meet education requirements, seminars, property tours)
- You time!

I even have them schedule their meals, exercise, and other activities.

Maher provides excellent resources for time-blocking your schedule, and there are sites online that help you customize and download calendars.

For me, a typical Monday looks like this:

5:00am: wake up and get ready for workout

5:30 - 6:35: workout

6:35 - 8:30: get ready for the day and eat breakfast, including 30 minutes on Facebook (SOCIAL MEDIA)

8:30 - 9: write thank you notes from OPEN HOUSE

9 - 10: set up client searches in MLS for current BUYERS/ people met at OPEN HOUSE; email those clients

10 - noon: scout neighborhood/house for upcoming LISTING appointment, take pictures of home/neighborhood

Noon - 1pm: eat lunch

1 - 4: meet with BUYERS to show homes, possibly write contract

4 - 5: write neighborhood blog post (INTERNET/SOCIAL MEDIA)

5 - 7: play with kids, have dinner

7 - 9: kids to bed, downtime, read business book, write journal entry

9pm: Sleep!

Each day of your week will be different. Some days you'll have coffee dates set up with your DATABASE. Other days you'll spend a couple of hours preparing for your OPEN HOUSE and another hour chatting with FSBOs and EXPIREDS. Mapping out your schedule brings you confidence and gives you direction so you don't feel like you're being pulled in opposite directions. And worse, if you don't have a road map for your day you may spend it doing unproductive things.

Agents who feel frustrated in this business don't map out their schedules. They wake up and either hustle and grind, hoping something they do will produce a sale, or they sit back and hope that business comes to them. With a clear plan of action in place, you know what you need to do each day and you can evaluate if the way you spent your time has been worthwhile. Having a schedule in place also helps you stay disciplined. How many times have you hopped onto Facebook *for just a minute*, looked at the clock, and hours have swept by? If you know you must log out at 8:30am so you can start your thank-you notes, you have established a disciplined system that keeps you accountable and on track.

Top-producing agents attribute their success to having a disciplined schedule; follow what successful agents do and you will be successful. Time-blocking and accountability systems are not new concepts in real estate. Successful agents don't simply hope that business comes their way, or grind away at time-wasting activities—they plan, and hold themselves accountable.

You are in charge of your schedule, which means you determine when you need to stick to your schedule and when it is okay to be flexible. For example, it's Monday and Amy Agent hasn't chosen her open house address yet, though when she set her weekly schedule earlier this morning she blocked out noon - 5pm on the upcoming Sunday for an open house (including set up/tear down). Her phone rings and a buyer would really like to see homes on Sunday. Does she immediately brush off the open house for her buyer, or does she stick to her plan of action? A buyer could mean a written contract, and an open house could mean a whole new handful of buyer and seller prospects.

If the buyer is local and not flying in and out over the weekend, Amy's strategic move is to show homes before or after the open house, making sure she has narrowed her buyer's list of homes to the three best (seeing more than three in a day is overwhelming for any buyer, regardless of what they think they can handle; set your clients' expectations in advance and help them make a wise decision by eliminating frustrations like showing too many homes in a day). This gives Amy adequate time to still do her open house. Choosing this route, she can help meet her buyer's needs, schedule additional homes for another day, and still prospect for clients at her open house. If Amy has church or another commitment Sunday morning, she'll only have time to show her buyer the three homes after the open house, and she'll need to plan a meal after the open house so she doesn't get weak. Her Sunday is now completely filled, including breaks, and now she knows that if she meets any red-hot buyers at the open house who want to view more homes in the neighborhood, she'll have to schedule them for another day. Through controlling her schedule she's able to pace herself and not get overwhelmed.

You need to understand that taking control of your schedule and setting boundaries for your clients and prospects is *okay*! People will respect your time more if you can respect your time. If a buyer throws a tantrum and must, absolutely, they'll die if they don't, see a home at a certain time, but you have another commitment, evaluate how real their desperation is and how you should best use your time. Does this buyer act like this every time they want to see a home? If yes, feel confident in continuing with your other commitment and demonstrate to your client that you have a schedule with set boundaries. "I have another appointment at 6pm, how does tomorrow work for you?" is an acceptable response, followed by a question that allows your buyer to still feel like a priority. However, if you know that your buyer is flying in just for the weekend, or if you two repeatedly face scheduling conflicts throughout the week and you truly cannot show them properties at another time, determine to go with the buyer and prospect another time. This is the value in being your own boss and having a flexible schedule.

A schedule helps you hold yourself accountable, but how do you stay disciplined? Even brokers or agents who are part of a team may not have a true feet-to-the-fire system in place. No matter what your set-up is in this business, have an accountability partner or mentor who holds you to your schedule.

Someone reading this is offended. That person, not you of course, scoffed, "I'm an independent agent/broker and do just fine without an accountability partner." In case you run into that 'self-sufficient' person, remind him that the most successful businesspeople of any generation have leaned on coaches and mentors. Look up any successful person: Richard Branson, Warren Buffet, Mark Zuckerberg, Sheryl Sandberg and Suze Orman have all had a mentor. If you want to be successful, do what the successful people do!

As a real estate professional you are an entrepreneur. Think about the one thing that separates entrepreneurs from employees: a boss. Even though you may have a broker who advises you and assumes some of your risk if a mistake is made during a transaction, *you* are ultimately responsible for your success. You don't have a boss to report to, or someone who will keep you on your toes and fire you when you underperform. While being boss-less sounds like a dream to entrepreneurially-minded people, you need to have some kind of accountability system in place to keep you on track. Partner with someone at your office, hire a coach, seek out a mentor—find someone you can commit to reporting to in lieu of having a boss to give you a level of discipline that is otherwise missing with entrepreneurship.

Tracking Your Success

Most agents consider their bank account as their tracking system. A padded account means they've been doing well, and overdrawn notices mean they need to up their hustle. The problem with this system is that it tracks the *past*. Your bank account is filled after a transaction closes, and if you're always looking at the past, you're not looking into the future. Deep, right?

Want to hear something that sends my super-organized

friends into a tizzy? I rarely check my bank account. I know, I know, this isn't really ideal since we should all keep tabs on our accounts to make sure we don't have any fraudulent activity (and I do check in from time to time so don't get any ideas!). But I don't need to stress out every day wondering if I have enough money in my account because I know, no matter what time of year it is, that I have a steady stream of money coming in. How do I know this? Because I track my success in a much more meaningful way.

Before I dive into the tracking system, I want to acknowledge that there are many software programs that help you track your success. This is not the platform to compare them. Find something you can use with ease; I'm a bit old school and a creature of habit, so I use the Excel program that came with my computer.

Once you find a system you know you'll stick with, create a sheet where you track the lead source for each of your closings. Have columns for the lead source (database, open house, etc.) and then rows where you attribute each closing address and commission received to the lead source. This is why I love the simplicity of Excel. I can easily keep a running sum under each lead source column and see how I'm performing in each category. Google Sheets makes it easy to share my tracking system with my partner and my mentor.

As an example, if the sum under my database column reads $80,000 in commission received and only $5,000 under the FSBO/Expired column, I now have a clear picture of what has been working for me (my database) and where I need to examine my efforts and make sure they are not lopsided (step up my FSBO game).

Your database column will usually be your top performer,

and this is the natural flow of real estate. You may meet a client at an open house, close them, keep them in your database, and then they contact you three years later to sell. Your client moved categories, from open house lead to database lead. Eventually you want to move everyone from their original category to database. The key is to make sure you keep adding people in the other categories so they can become database members as past clients and continual referral sources for you!

Address	Database	Internet/ Social Media	Farming	Open Houses	FSBOs/ Expireds	Referrals	Other
123 Main St.	$6,000						
237 West St.			$9,000				
19 River Oaks	$15,000						
2726 Lakefront						$10,000	
90 Silver Trail				$10,500			
Sum	**$21,000**		**$9,000**	**$10,500**		**$10,000**	

(For a template, visit http://www.ShannonEnsor.com/ realestatemachine/resources/)

If you see a category you are underperforming in, analyze your schedule and the time spent prospecting for clients in that category. Look for ways to pump up your time in that area, while not taking away from your success-producing activities. In the short example above, closings from FSBO and Internet leads are lacking, but open houses and farming have produced closings. You wouldn't want to cut out the open houses to find time for your FSBOs, but rather look for holes in your schedule so you can improve upon this weak spot.

Tracking your successes is paramount to achieving a well-rounded career. You may think, *but if I'm doing well without FSBOs, then why should I even bother?* Sure, you may have a great business in place, with sufficient income, but you're leaving money on the table! If you knew you could make simple tweaks to your schedule to ensure that your career is performing at optimal levels, you wouldn't be okay with leaving money on the table, would you? Prevent the valleys in your income stream by monitoring and adjusting your strengths and weaknesses, and you'll see your income rise on an ever-steady incline. When you track your successes and uncover areas that are closing-deficient, you determine how to make them as strong as your other components. Do not continue lop-sided just because you *seem* to be trucking along just fine without the adjustment.

We real estate professionals have a common mantra we say to clients. They ask, "If I buy this house, will I be able to sell it for more money in five years?" or they might ask, "Do you think I should buy now or wait until after the 'season' to see if prices go down?" And we all answer, "Sorry, if only I had a crystal ball I could help you out there!" Of course, we help educate them on the pros and cons of their decision and leave them with more than a consoling pat on the back, but I'm betting this saying is familiar to you. Well, when it comes to *your* success, you actually do have a crystal ball!

Let me explain. When you track your lead sources, continually monitoring for weak spots and making adjustments, you can predict your income for at least three months out, and arguably longer. For example, let's say you met with a business coach three years ago and began implementing the time-blocked schedule. In the first year post-implementation you earned $100,000. In year two you earned $125,000, and in year three you earned $156,250, which means you increased your income by 25% year after year through the process of scheduling, accountability and adjusting. If you analyze your data and see that each year, 60% of your income comes from your database, 20% comes from open houses, 10% comes from farming and 10% comes from referrals, you can surmise that if you continue the process of scheduling, accountability, and adjusting, you should have another 25% increase in income next year.

But we don't prefer to look ahead one year from now. Instead, we tend to focus on three-month intervals. *How many closings do I have coming up?* So let's break it down further. If you know that 60% of your closings last month came from your database, and your weekly schedule allows you to spend 30% of your time nurturing your database and another 30% of your time showing homes or presenting them with listing appointments, the same as you did the previous month, you will be on track to make the same 60% of your income each month, for the next three months, because of your database.

Agents operate on a rolling three-month time frame due to the nature of real estate sales—some transactions take longer to close, some fall through—so what happens today can affect your bank account from one to three months from now (or even longer with new home sales). But if you keep identifying your weaknesses and turning them into strengths, then you know your rolling three months should continue to be as good as or better than the last month. Your ratios may stay the same (60% database, 20% open house, etc.), but the income will gradually grow as your database and influence does.

Leveraging Components and Working Smarter

We're not going to wake up tomorrow and find that open houses are obsolete. Farming will always be a powerful way to dominate a neighborhood. You're going nowhere in this business without a database. The Internet and social media are here to stay. The six tried-and-true components discussed in this book encompass what you need to do in this business to be successful. To work smarter you need to implement all six components *together*.

Buyers and Sellers. I'll start here since this is not the typical weak spot for an agent. Most agents I know will drop anything for a chance to drive around a buyer, or get a "For Sale" sign up in yard. (Although I did have a team member turn down a $500,000-buyer because she had to show a low income housing-qualified lease applicant one house. On one hand, I commend her for following through on her commitment to that tenant—and I get it, if you've shown someone a ton of houses already that haven't worked out, you *really* want the next house to work out so you can get paid and move on. But personally I would have politely asked for a rain check or shuffled my schedule by an hour so that I could get paid $15,000 instead of $225!)

When you time-block your schedule, allot times to meet with clients each day and notice over time what tends to work best for you, and where your scheduling conflicts seem to arise. Every client will present different scheduling challenges, and you can't control that. But what you can control is creating a well-thought-through schedule that allows you to roll with their challenges and still have time to prospect for new clients.

If you see a pattern of scratching through your open house preparation time on Tuesdays so that you can meet with buyers, but your Fridays always seem unproductive, rearrange your schedule to maximize your time each Friday so that open houses don't get put on the back burner. If you're feeling burnt-out because your buyers keep intruding on your scheduled YOU-time, then analyze your schedule and see how you can accommodate your clients without losing yourself.

If getting buyers and sellers to the closing table is your weakness, you need to determine whether it's due to lack of prospecting for those clients, or if you are unable to close those leads once you have them. What other components do you need to integrate into your business so you can get in front of more leads? If you're good at gathering leads, but can't close them once you have them, you either need to be more active with your leads (all leads funnel to your database and increase your interaction with your database) or you need to become a better salesperson.

First, do you exude the confidence of a professional salesperson, and do you have a branding package that transfers your confidence into all the material you pass out to your leads? Second, ask your leads open-ended questions and genuinely listen to their responses. Your objective for each conversation is to get to the listing appointment or schedule a day of touring homes together. Finally, if you have clients but they aren't closing, you'll need to set some realistic expectations. For example, if your listing isn't selling, find out why and tackle that problem with your seller. Or if your buyer won't get off the fence on buying, have the heart-to-heart with them about why they wanted to buy in the first place and see if their emotional goals line up with their financial goals.

Database. As I've mentioned, when you track your leads you'll see that a good deal of closings are the result of nurturing your database. If you notice that you've been database-poor, either in terms of how large your database is or in terms of closings, you need to schedule more time each week for growing and nurturing your database. You can find many "database memory jogger" lists online. The last time I had my team members fill out a memory-jogger, an agent who already had a database of a few hundred, and thought he couldn't possibly add more, added more than 60 people he hadn't previously thought of!

Your database is your sweet spot in this business, so make sure you have time set aside each week to nurture your database. Here are a few tips:

- Aim to send handwritten notes to five different database members each week.
- Make one coffee date per week with someone in your database.
- Make one lunch date per week with someone in your database.
- Make it a habit to accept invitations from your database: go to happy hours, social events.
- Comment sincerely on ten of your Facebook friends' posts per day.
- Call one person from your database each week.

These are some ideas that can help boost your database closing ratios. Adjust them to fit *you*, not me. Perhaps you are a phone person and abhor Facebook—then call five people per week to see how they are doing.

Then, make sure you are adding everyone from your open

houses and farm to your database. If an Internet lead comes through, or someone comments on a blog post and you receive their email address, add them to your database. Every FSBO and expired seller needs to be in your database, too. Every component and tactic should feed directly into your database.

If you see that you are neglecting your database at any point, jump back in and get in front of them. Your time and money is always well-spent when it comes to the people who already have the inclination to want to do business with you!

Internet/Social Media. Are you poor in leads from your website or social media accounts? First, do you have a personal website capable of receiving leads? Do you have a Facebook business page where you can run ads? Once you have those established, you need to spend a small amount of time each week throwing fish nets into the water and catching leads.

Action items to catch more Internet leads:

- Write one blog post per week on a neighborhood that you would like to feature. Bonus: this neighborhood should somehow be connected to your farm or an open house so you can amplify your efforts. Make sure to have a call to action so prospects can contact you.
- Link your blog to your social media accounts. Run ads (refer to your budget) so you can catch leads.
- Post videos online (YouTube, then share to your social media or do the Facebook Live videos) with you giving industry advice, or simply touring a community.
- Post about your upcoming open houses.
- Feature small business owners in/near your farm.
- Determine your budget for Google ads that you can run

yourself without needing to hire a company, and your Facebook ads. Run ads on your listings or home search pages from your site.

- Create Facebook groups for the neighborhood you farm—invite FSBOs and expired leads to your groups so they can see your interaction with their community and view you as a the neighborhood expert.

You'll notice that many of these items should not take very much of your time each week and can be done in only a couple of hours. Make sure you have scheduled these hours each week and adjust accordingly as you become more proficient, and the steps become second nature to you. You'll find that areas on your schedule begin to overlap as you're working on one component (like open house marketing) that also works to build another component (receiving Internet leads from your open house blog posts).

Farming. If you haven't yet invested in a farming program, you'll definitely have deficits in this column. Identify a budget that you can apply to a farm, even if it means you are starting small. You can always increase your farm as your budget grows.

What if you have been plugging away at a farm with no return? Is your marketing material branded to you, or to your brokerage? How long have you been sending out your material, and how consistently? Your farming material <u>must</u> be branded to you and sent on a consistent basis, forever.

Use the power of the other components in your business to leverage your farming success:

- When you're working with <u>buyers and sellers </u>in your farm, shout out about it on your <u>social media</u> accounts.

- Be sure to utilize "Just Listed" and "Just Sold" postcards to boost your credibility as a producing agent.
- Members from your SOI that reside in your farm are your superstars. Make sure to contact them regularly.
- Create Facebook groups for your farm. This can be a general neighborhood page or more specific sub-pages (mom groups, fitness-minded groups, buy/sell/trade groups).
- Be sure to have blog posts and videos about your farm that also feature you out and about in your farm. Feature local events, business owners and unique features of the community (such as hiking trails) in your videos and posts. Post these on your personal website and your social media accounts.
- Blast your farm with open house invitations. You should focus your open houses in your farm. Your branded open house directionals should become fixtures in your farm, giving you undeniable presence in the community.
- Connect face-to-face with every seller from the FSBO and expired listings in your farm. Your desire to have complete knowledge of your farm is your warm foot in the door with these sellers.
- Hold networking and social events in your farm, as well as seminars.

When you use the strategies above and view your farm as an opportunity to become famous in your target area, rather than simply a monthly financial obligation when the postcards go out, you start to get excited about this component. The more you show up as the neighborhood expert and can be seen in front of your farm, the more the leads will start to pour in, resulting in greater closings.

Open Houses. If you notice a lack of leads coming from open houses, you first need to determine if this is because you do not *do* enough open houses, or if you are not doing them the correct way.

You should aim for 40 open houses per year. If you meet at least four people at each open house, at 40 open houses per year, you can add 160 leads a year from open houses alone! If you close only 10% of those leads, that still means 16 closings will come from open houses each year. Not bad, eh? If all 16 homes you close have $200,000 sales prices, you'll conceivably earn $96,000/year just from your open houses. Convinced you need to schedule more time for your open houses yet?

If you've been holding homes open, but haven't received the level of success explained in the formula above, you aren't doing them correctly. You will schedule blocks of time each week on Tuesdays, Thursdays or Fridays, a few minutes on Saturdays, and then several hours on Sundays for open houses. I go into great detail about open houses in *Your Key to Open House Success*, but in the meantime, here are some tips to help you achieve more success in your open houses:

- Hold your open houses in an area you want to farm to maximize your neighborhood exposure and credibility.
- Invite neighbors and tell them to invite friends and co-workers.
- Give incentives for signing in, such as a drawing for a gift card that will later be announced on your Facebook business page.

- Talk to FSBOs and expireds in the neighborhood of your open house so you are armed with knowledge, and can build rapport with those sellers.

- Blog about your open house and run ads on your business page to help get the blog in front of new Internet leads while showing your current fans that you're an agent who takes action!

FSBOs/Expireds. If the words FSBO and expireds make you cringe, that's probably because you associate them with cold-calling or cold-knocking. I know many agents who love the cold approach, but not me. I also know that many agents spend an hour or two every morning putting together mailers to send to these seller leads. I've been there and decided it wasn't worth my time or budget. I *know* that agents can be successful with those methods, but I prefer to go another route. And if you notice that you lack closings in this area, then you may like my approach, too.

- Contact FSBOs/expireds in the neighborhood you are holding an open house in—use the warm approach that you'd like to get more information about the home in case your open house visitors inquire.

- Give FSBOs/expireds a no-obligation chance to be featured in your farming material, including your website/social media. This builds your rapport with them and puts you at the top of their list when they are ready to list/re-list.

- Add FSBOs/expireds that you've made contact with to your database.

Both of these methods present you with a valid reason to build a relationship with sellers, taking out the cold-factor completely.

Did you see a pattern with each of these sections? Each component intertwines with and enhances another. When you prepare for your open house throughout the week, you are also reaching out to your farm, your social media, and to FSBOs/expireds—and the pattern continues within each component. Suddenly, the daunting task of creating your schedule is alleviated because you can use one area of your business to boost another. Separately, all the tasks could overwhelm you, but when you learn to work these areas together, your real estate machine begins to run smoothly and you are no longer running in circles wondering what you should be doing to become successful. Identify your weaknesses and schedule time each week to develop them into income-producing strengths!

Chapter 11
Attitude and Environment

WHEN YOU AND YOUR BANK ACCOUNT start to feel the effects of a well-rounded, smooth-running real estate business, your attitude will shift from frustrated, hopeless and stuck to positive, confident and focused. You'll notice that your new attitude will begin to attract new business for you, because people are attracted to positive people and prefer to do business with someone who is happy and confident.

A bad attitude does nothing for you except to create obstacles to success. Be aware of your attitude at all times, even when you think no one is watching (yep, that means no throwing hammers into the street and kicking your open house directional sign when it refuses to go in the ground). Prospective clients will run away if you display even the slightest bad attitude.

You are more likely to let your guard down in front of friends and family, people who are also members of your database (your SOI), and they are even quicker to judge you if you seem unpleasant to work with. If they hear you complaining all the time about work, they're not going to want to be a part of your 'problem.' Don't turn away people, especially your database, with a bad attitude.

Who would you hire to sell your home if you weren't in this business? With their qualifications being equal, would you hire the agent who exuded passion for her job or the one who grumbled and complained about the market? The answer is obvious. Make sure you're the former, not the latter.

I cringe when I hear agents practically shoot themselves in the foot when they vent about their business. In a friendly conversation they're asked, "How's business going?" With no filter, the agent responds, "Oh, horrible! None of my buyers can win a bid in this multiple-offer market and somehow I'm stuck with the only listings that can't sell right now. It's no cakewalk being in real estate!" The agent wants consoling, and perhaps to convey that they've been working hard, and the other person will feel sorry for them all right—and move on to a more enthusiastic agent when they're ready to buy or sell.

Here's another scenario that comes back to haunt agents. A non-agent will comment, "Real estate seems like such a fun industry to be in! I've been thinking about getting my license." The agent rears back and unleashes every negative thought she can conjure about the business in order to dissuade a potential future competitor. She lets her fear of competition affect her attitude. When that friend puts her dream of becoming an agent on the back-burner, but hears of a co-worker who needs to sell their home and relocate within the city, she doesn't refer the co-worker to her angry agent/friend who seemed to hate her job the last time they spoke. Don't let a bad attitude get in the way of your success!

Keeping Your Glow

I've given you strategies to form a well-rounded business, and as you've read I'm sure you realized there hasn't been one shortcut or secret recipe that requires no work or effort on your part. You must have a can-do attitude in this business and the willingness to do the work required if you want to become successful. Because you are taking the time to invest in yourself and in your career by reading this book, I believe that you have that can-do attitude already. But how do you keep that new-agent glow when you've suffered a few scrapes and bruises in the business? Incorporate the following into your life:

- Exercise and live a healthy lifestyle. Hundreds of thousands of books have been written about how exercise and a healthy diet/lifestyle positively affect you. There's a reason why these topics are so popular. Make it a priority to exercise at least four to five days a week; the blood flow and endorphins alone will help push you through a bad day at the office. I prefer to start off my day with exercise, but if a stressful situation occurs later in the day, you'll surely see me hitting the streets for a jog to let my nerves calm down. Bonus: joining a group fitness program introduces you to new clients!
- Social/family/down-time. It's easy for agents to get so wrapped up in their day-to-day tasks that they never take the time for themselves. I recently had to ban laptops at the dinner table. Nothing says "I love you"

like an entire meal spent catching up on emails—said no one ever. Most agents say they got into this business because they wanted more freedom and more time with their families, only to find they ignore their families for work. It's easy to do, and you may not even notice it happening until after you hit burn-out and are lugging around a bad attitude. Be cognizant of how much time you're spending on yourself and your loved ones, and make sure you truly are enjoying life and the freedom of working for yourself. Doing so will keep you energized and ready to tackle your career with a positive attitude!

- Remember your *why*. Why did you get into real estate? To work for yourself? Great! The next time you're frustrated, think about the freedoms you have by running your own business. Does it feel like you *don't* have any freedom? Then it's time to restructure your schedule (go back to Chapter 10, on implementation).

Did you get into this business to help people, but the stresses from your transactions are making that dream seem fuzzy? Reach out to your past clients and ask them to help you update your online reviews. Their comments will lift up your spirits and remind you of your *why*.

Did you become an agent because you really love design and making homes beautiful? Perhaps you're in the right industry, but wearing the wrong hat. Shadow a stager for a few months and decide if you need to make a shift in the industry, or if your heart really yearns to be an agent. The experience will help renew your spirit and the focus on direction will reinforce your glow.

Warding off Negativity

You can be the most positive person in the world, but when surrounded by negative people it can be hard to keep on the bright side of things. As real estate professionals we are targets of negative generalizations—"Oh, you're a *realator* (that pronunciation is my biggest pet peeve!), what, couldn't make it as a used car salesman?"—and of misguided curiosity.

When I first joined the business my grandmother, one of my most favorite people on this planet, would ask me every week, "Did you sell a house yet?" Her question wore at me—and this was only a few weeks into the business. Unbeknownst to her, the constant questioning drove me to make my first sale happen so I could finally answer, "Yes!" Of course her question then became, "How many houses have you sold?" She meant well, and while the questions helped motivate me to succeed, they also gave me a lot of self-doubt. I have a strong 'prove 'em wrong' mentality that drives me to succeed. (Want to be my best friend? Act like you don't like me and I'll set out to prove you wrong!) Even if we don't have this in common, the questions may still eat away at your positive attitude and cause you to question your profession.

Prevent this from happening by understanding why people question you. The real reason behind their questions may be jealousy, because they've always wished to become their own boss and have an exciting career with ever-changing scenery. Respond to their questions positively and then let it roll off your shoulders. You don't need to worry about *their* why, only they do.

Sometimes it's harder to escape the negativity. Some agents, mostly those who are struggling, experience tension from a spouse who discourages them from continuing in real estate. With licensing and brokerage fees and the multitude of marketing costs, this is not a cheap business to get into. But *no* business is free to start up! Have a heart-to-heart with your honey and make sure your family is all on the same page when it comes to finances, budgeting, and goals. Show them your schedule and action plans.

When I see an agent on my team who is discouraged at home, and I can see the negativity taking a toll on their performance, I meet with the spouse separately and discuss the agent's future. I tell them they need to be more supportive if they want their spouse to succeed in real estate and explain that their negativity is a huge roadblock to that success. I make sure to outline the paths to success their agent-spouse has been taking, and where I see them in one to two years if they keep on their projection. This usually helps the doubting-spouse to back down and take a more supportive role. If you are experiencing this, talk to your broker and see if they can have a heart-to-heart with your loved one. Once your spouse sees what you're doing to ensure you have a successful career, they can be more supportive. It is worth the effort to save your career.

Your Company Matters

Is the company you've chosen to work with (or the principles of the company you've built) conducive to *your* success?

Are you in a positive environment? Does it encourage ideas, sharing, and networking between agents? It's true, you are an independent agent, but your environment can certainly affect you. As an agent, the time I spend in my brick and mortar office is minimal. When clients ask me where my office is located, I tell them with a wink, "In my car at any point in this city." However, it is good to know that when I do need to be at my office, it's an environment I enjoy being in . . . and you need that enjoyment, as well.

I'm privileged to work in an environment where agents freely share ideas. The referral rate within our mid-size brokerage is outstanding. We don't worry about agents stealing our ideas and clients or back-stabbing. I attribute this to our president and his high hiring standards. Look for these elements when you're searching for a brokerage to call home.

Here's a biggie: Are you encouraged to brand yourself, or are you forced to stick with your company's logo only? If you are not allowed or encouraged to build your brand, then stop what you are doing and find another brokerage to work with immediately. The best way to stick out in consumers' minds is to uniquely brand you. If you spend money to mail postcards to your farm each month, sweat each weekend as you drive your open house directionals into the ground, and pay for your own web hosting, not only should you receive the benefits of that work, but the only way to maximize the effectiveness of those efforts is through branding yourself.

For example, two agents send postcards to an apartment complex every month talking about the benefits of homeownership—the same generic card written by an advertising agency, but there is space for agents to personalize the card. Agent A has his *company's* logo all over the card, and Agent B has his *personal* logo, headshot, and short, fun bio about himself.

One of the recipients decides it's time to buy a home and since she doesn't have an agent, she thinks about the postcards she regularly gets in the mail. Who do you think she will call? The chances are in favor of Agent B who stuck out in the renter's mind due to his unique logo and personal bio, which she had skimmed a few times over the last several months on the way to the trash can. Let's go to the worse-case scenario and say the renter didn't like something about Agent B's face—hey, it happens! But she remembers also receiving postcards from another *brokerage*. She can't remember the agent's name, just the company logo that flashed past her eyes as the postcard went from mailbox to trashcan. She searches for the company name online and gives the front desk a call. Agent A wasn't on phone duty that day, so another agent got the lead.

This is so important, it's worth repeating: brand yourself. If someone in your audience doesn't call because they didn't like your face, that's their issue and probably best you don't work with them anyway! At least you know you did your part to stand out in your audience's mind and **you** will receive more calls from the branding. It beats driving leads to the phone duty desk, where you may not be sitting, any day.

This leads me to my final question: **Are you in business for yourself or do you work for another agent/team?** If you work on a team, you may feel like you have job security, but what happens if the team breaks up, or your team leader moves or has to get out of the business altogether? Have you branded *yourself* to the clients you were given, or only your team leader's name? Put a game plan in place. Know how to work a balanced business that incorporates the methods in this book so you don't have to start over as a new agent if your team disbands.

Maybe you are a team leader or broker reading this and you're thinking, "Hey! Don't tell my agents not to brand *me* or to think about *their* best interests as an individual agent!" Get that fear out of your head now. Clients become more connected to their agent than the company they work for. Let your agents build their brand so they *can* be more memorable in clients' minds—thus making them, and you, more successful. If you hold your agents back, they will eventually want to break away, so give them the freedom now and both of your careers will benefit from it.

Lastly, make sure you are with a company that is on the forefront of what is new in the industry. Allow your mentors to weed through the latest and greatest and the fads (QR codes anyone?) so that you can stay focused on prospecting. When your mentors find something worth incorporating into your business and suggest you jump on board, you know you are with the right company.

You've learned the necessary components of a successful business and that the right attitude and the right environment unhinge obstacles that prevent you from taking action. Now it's time to take action!

Chapter 12
Take Action!

THERE IS A REASON WHY EVERY coach and mentor preaches that writing down your goals is a good success tool. Writing your goals, physically seeing them and revisiting what expectations you have set for yourself, helps keep you motivated.

Many fitness gurus say not to look at the scale when you're trying to lose weight, to instead gauge your success by how your pants fit. Every time I shun the scale, though, I fall off the wagon big-time. However, when I weigh in every morning and actually see the numbers, I hold myself more accountable to my goals and can either celebrate successes or realize I need to increase my discipline. The same goes for your career. Write down your goals so you can continually revisit them, celebrate your successes, and know when you need to step it up. If you simply rely on how your pants fit, or how your bank account looks, you can veer off track and may not even realize it until it is too late.

Here are the questions to ask yourself, and get out your pen! Be specific with your answers, and your goals:

What was your income last year from real estate sales?	
Where would you like your income to be this year?	
Where would you like your income to be the following year?	
How many buyers did you work with last year?	
How many buyers will you need to work with this year in order to hit your income goal?	
How many sellers did you work with last year?	
How many sellers will you need to work with this year in order to hit your income goal?	
What is your list-to-close ratio? (If you sell four out of every five homes you list, and your goal is to list/sell 20 homes this year, know that you need to procure 25 listings.)	
How many people are in your database?	
If you'd like to increase your income by 10% this year, aim to increase your database by 10%. What is your new target number for your database?	
How many Internet leads did you receive last year?	
How many will you need to get this year to hit your goal?	
How many open houses did you do last year?	
How many open houses should you do this year to hit your goal? 40?	
How many FSBOs did you turn into clients last year?	
How many FSBOs will you need to talk to this year to hit your goal?	
How many expired listings did you turn into personal listings last year?	
How many expired listings do you need this year to hit your goal?	

Reach higher each year with your goals. Push yourself to beat your previous year's numbers.

Now you know what numbers you need in order to hit your goals. Post your goals somewhere you can see them every day—your desktop wallpaper, or a print version framed above your desk. Then send them to your mentor and tell them you'd like assistance holding your feet to the fire with these goals.

Next, plan what you need to do each week to hit them. If you know you need to increase your open houses from 20 per year to 40 per year, pre-fill your schedule three months in advance with time blocked for your open houses, including the preparation days. If you know you need to double your Internet leads, schedule check-in points every other week to analyze your online ads budget and gauge if the ads are producing results.

It doesn't matter if you are reading this in the middle of the year or on December 31st. There is no time like the present to begin your goal-setting and goal-hitting. Don't wait until "the right time"—it doesn't exist. Life is crazy and there is never a more perfect time than right now to shape your career into the satisfying and successful one it is meant to be! Begin methodically growing your business through purposeful prospecting now, so your tomorrow is better than yesterday.

When you set this book down, get started on your career right away. Don't put it off. Print out a calendar and begin your schedule **now**. Take each component, one-by-one, and integrate them into your schedule. Come back to your schedule every morning and night so you can stay on track and evaluate if you are putting in the work to hit your goals. Soon it will become second nature for you to evaluate your schedule, and a kind of addiction to seeing results in your income forms. Maybe you're working hard and still your closings are a few weeks away, so your bank account looks meager. That's okay. Your daily tracking shows you that things are about to change.

Keep in mind the pie piece with your prospecting goals. The viscous cycle of falling flat after each closing, not knowing where your next lead is coming from stops **now**. Work each area congruently so that you have a steady flow of business at all times.

Appendix
Additional Success Tips

Here are some tips for giving exceptional service that will earn you referrals and repeat business:

Tips for working with buyers and sellers:

- Build trust and rapport with your clients. Make sure they know you are on their side no matter what (following ethics and Fair Housing Laws, of course) and that their goals are your goals.

- Ask buyers open-ended questions when showing homes. Allow the process to open up their minds about each home rather than checking a box and running off to see the next home on the list. Open-ended questions can help them come to a decision faster and they will feel like they made the best decision for themselves.

- I still prefer to drive clients in my own car when possible. Always make sure your car looks and smells great. Even if I'm not driving, I always bring cold bottled water and snacks for everyone in tow (including extended family who are merely along to interject opinions).

- Preview your route and homes before showing buyer clients; you will look more professional and be able to offer more input instead of spending time getting lost or hunting down lockboxes. Previewing also helps you offer advice to clients, "Oh, if you've decided you don't like sunken living rooms, then maybe we should cross off the next two homes on the list and spend more time at the house on the corner you were really excited about seeing." Yes, you will need to schedule time for previewing.

- Prepare helpful numbers for lenders, home warranty companies, inspectors, etc., and keep them handy <u>before</u> they have to ask you for them. Hand them a print copy and email them an electronic one that's not so easy to lose. Understand that clients may not be as responsible with the paperwork you give them as you would hope; never begrudge a second or tenth request for paperwork you know you already sent them.

- Learn to say and spell their names correctly. Sounds simple, but you'd be surprised at how often agents mess this up!

- Give thoughtful closing gifts. A gift card is always welcomed, but not always memorable. Think through your conversations with them—is there something specific you can pick up on? For example, maybe your clients had always dreamed of having a pool and are finally getting one. Give them pool accessories as a closing gift.

- Throw your buyers a housewarming party, and your

sellers a going-away party. Both are excellent ways to grow your database, especially when your client raves about you in front of everyone at the party. Many lenders are happy to share in the catering expenses of the party, too!

- Learn expert negotiation tactics so that your clients know they are working with the best of the best. I highly recommend the Certified Negotiation Expert course.

- Pay for staging boot camp for <u>all</u> of your sellers, whether the house is already magazine-worthy or a complete fixer-upper. When your clients know that *everyone* receives this service from you, they will feel confident in referring you to their friends and family.

- Always, always, always get professional photography! There is absolutely no excuse these days not to have it! If your other business is not professional photography, you are not a professional photographer!

- Be active in your marketing—never let listings get stale. Have agents hold your listings open; organize neighborhood-wide open houses. Place your home on broker tours and share the feedback with your sellers. Communicate early and often with your sellers so they know what you are doing to sell their home. It's better for them to get tired of hearing from you than for them to never hear from you at all.

- Be proactive for your buyers. Their 'perfect' home doesn't exist in the MLS? Advertise your buyer's needs to other brokerages and look for pocket listings. Contact FSBOs and expireds for your buyers. Let them know what you are doing behind the scenes on their behalf! This creates the most loyal buyers who will send you countless referrals. And you may pick up some listings from the FSBOs and expireds in the process!

- Don't forget about your clients after closing. Not only should they be a part of your database, but they should hear from you on birthdays and holidays. Set dates throughout the year to contact past clients: for example, in January call everyone whose last name begins with A-B; February C-D; March E-F; and so on. Ask them to coffee or remember something specific about their lives to talk to them about (ask about their child's swim meet, for example, rather than if they know of anyone looking to buy or sell).

Tips for nurturing and growing your database:
- Every night, think about who you met and can add to your database.
- Categorize your database so you can focus your efforts more heavily on your star members.
- National holidays make great excuses to reach out to your database, but surprise them randomly with "calling for no reason other than to see how I can help you."
- Commit to emailing a newsletter once a month. Follow the 80/20 rule with the content of your newsletter: 80% should be content that appeals to *them*, 20% should be about you/your listings/open houses.
- Ever have someone randomly pop into your head? When that happens, stop what you're doing (if you can,

or make a mental note to do this later if you cannot) and reach out to that person. It's that simple.

- Your database feeling a bit light? Join some local groups to start amping it up! Enjoy working out? Join fitness groups. Be active in your PTA or church. Work the other areas of your business, such as open houses, in order to grow your database. Go where the people are and start introducing yourself!

Tips for building your business through Internet/ social media leads:

- Being online helps keep you in front of potential buyers and sellers—help them remember you over your competition!
- Always have a CTA! Let people know they *need* to contact you, and give them the how-to.
- Make sure your email signature points people to your social media sites and website. Test your links regularly to make sure they are still working.
- When meeting someone new, be sure to like or follow them on social media. You hope that they will follow you back, but don't become discouraged or pushy when they don't.
- Run out of blog content ideas? Look into neighborhoods that are considered move-up or move-down in regards to your farm.
- Fresh video and blog content can also come from other real estate professionals, such as interviews with lenders, title company agents, inspectors and stagers.

- Beware of over-posting outbound links on your Facebook page. Sure, it's great that you are pointing to major articles written by others that your followers may find enjoyable, but those links don't help people connect to *you*.

- Don't be afraid to let your personality shine! Are you a leather-wearing, tattoo-sporting, motorcycle-driving agent? Or are you a mom of two beautiful children who are your world? Show your followers! They connect with you better and you'll have long-term stickability with them because of your personality. I'm the latter of the two personalities, and have loyal clients who are the former. Your personalities don't have to be the same, ***your*** personality just has to stick out!

Farming tips:
- Choose a location that you are passionate about and stay there. Bouncing from farm to farm slows your momentum.

- Consistently mail to your farm once a month, but don't stop there. Let the other areas of your business boost your presence in your farm and enhance your neighborhood credibility.

- If you're spending money on advertising, advertise in your farm to get more for your money. Every piece must be branded to you.

- Postcards leave more of an impression than sealed envelopes.

- Contact people in your farm and see how you can help

them and their community. For example, if they wish they had a lending library, be the one to set it up.

- Give POV (Pieces of Value) to your farm. Mix up fun holiday pieces with market stats. Let them know you are the source for all things real estate in your community.
- Business owners in your farm are the most influential members—find out how you can help promote each other.

Open house tips:
- Check out the detailed day-by-day marketing plan for open houses in *Your Key to Open House Success*.
- You are marketing yourself just as much as the listing at each open house. Be sure to put your best foot forward when it comes to your appearance, and the appearance of the material and treats you pass out to guests.
- Partner with a lender to raise the professionalism at your open houses.
- Brand your directional signs and aim to post at least 10 in order to increase your traffic.
- Ask local businesses if they'll allow you to place an open house invite where customers can see it.
- Worried about those leftover treats? Package them nicely and bring them to the closest fire or police station, or a school office, along with a flyer about loan programs for those professions.
- Create a video of you announcing the winner of your open house drawing and post to your social media accounts. Let visitors know to "like" your page so they

can see the announcement (of course, you'll want
to contact the winners personally as well).

Tips for warming up FSBOs and expireds:

- FSBOs and expireds don't have to be approached in
  the cold-call manner. Use open houses to get yourself in
  the door of these skeptical sellers and you'll earn their
  respect—and business—as the neighborhood expert.
- Buyers *want* to know about FSBOs/expireds, so it is
  your duty to be knowledgeable! There is no trickery
  involved with this warm method. Therefore, shake
  off any nerves and approach these leads with
  confidence and a genuine smile.
- Place FSBO/expired leads that you've warmly contacted
  in your database. Make sure they receive your open
  house invitations and "Just Sold" postcards.
- Create FSBO packages to leave with sellers after your
  first conversation. The package should include important
  state disclosures, your personal marketing material and
  a piece explaining how FSBOs typically sell for *less* than
  homes listed with REALTORS®.

About the Author

Shannon Ensor has been an Austin REALTOR® since 2005, and has earned titles and designations that include Broker, Accredited Buyer's Representative, Graduate Realtor Institute and Certified Negotiation Expert. In addition to being a top-producing agent, she has mentored a team of agents since 2009. She expands her passion for mentoring agents and for real estate in her books, ensuring that agents around the world have access to the knowledge they need to succeed. In each book she writes, she holds nothing back and gives her readers every secret, strategy and tactic she has learned over her years of building a successful real estate career. Through her experiences with mentoring agents, Shannon has also learned the go-to objections agents create that sabotage their success. She passes along her sabotage-proof mindset to her readers and hopes that each one will gain the knowledge and motivation to become the best agent they can possibly be.

www.ShannonEnsor.com
www.facebook.com/shannonensorbooks
www.twitter.com/shannon_ensor

Other books by Shannon

Your Key to Open House Success

Stop Wasting Your Time on Property Tours (FREE ebook!)

Amp up your open house game!

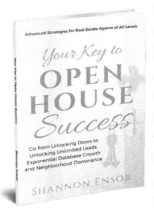

Learn more than 100 tips and strategies to turn your open houses into lead generating, database growing, and credibility building events! Your Key to Open House Success gives you a day-by-day guide to marketing your open houses and how you can position yourself in each step to grow your business! http://www.ShannonEnsor.com

"I am a new Realtor. I held an open house for another agent about a month ago and was at a loss to how and what I was doing. Needless to say, it did not turn out well. I bought this book and am so glad I did! Shannon has not only given the steps to how to have a very successful open house, but wonderful information on growing your database before, during and after! This is a must read for every Realtor that wants to be successful in growing their business! Thank you Shannon!" – Becky Erdek, Naples, FL

CPSIA information can be obtained
at www.ICGtesting.com
Printed in the USA
BVHW03s0830290318
511937BV00001B/48/P